185 DAYS

185 DAYS
School Stories

Linda Ball

ORANGE *frazer* PRESS
Wilmington, Ohio

ISBN 9781939710-192

Published for the author by:
Orange Frazer Press
P.O. Box 214
Wilmington, OH 45177
Telephone: 800.852.9332 for price and shipping information.
Website: www.orangefrazer.com
www.orangefrazercustombooks.com

Book and cover design: Alyson Rua and Orange Frazer Press
Cover art painting by Johann Zoffany

Library of Congress Control Number 2014953814

Dedicated to my parents

Jane and John Ludwig

Acknowledgements

Thanks to all the women at Women Writing for (a) Change. Without their advice and encouragement this book would never have reached completion.

Introduction

You'll never see an article in the newspaper about me, the featured teacher in a classroom that works. I'll never be selected Teacher of the Year, and I don't make a difference. No student ever told me I was his favorite teacher. I'm not cool, I have no charisma, and there's no warm and fuzzy atmosphere in Room 233. I am two generations older than my students, an anachronism, a lady who attempts to keep teenagers from their social lives, cigarettes, cell-phones, and iPods from 8 a.m. to 3 p.m. every Monday through Friday, 185 days a year.

Forget that I am always at work, punctual and prepared, and that in 30 years of teaching I have used less than ten sick days. I keep up with progressive techniques such as role play, interactive computer lessons, and power point presentations, but no one seems to notice or care. No one appreciates the fact that I supply the room with Band-Aids, hard candy for sore throats, pens, pencils, paper, and notebooks. I especially resent how students abuse my Kleenex. I buy boxes with my own money, graciously set them on the window sill, then watch kids blow their noses and drop the dirty tissues on the floor. When I ask them to use the garbage can, they say, "It wasn't me," and walk out of the room. My two master's degrees have qualified me to pick up hazardous waste after teens.

It serves me right. I didn't get into teaching because of any altruistic passion to uplift and enlighten children. When I signed up for my college courses, teaching was the most practical career choice. My only philanthropic notions were toward myself. I had a burning desire to be a golf pro, but Dad said I had to go to college first. If I didn't make it on the pro tour, I would have my degree to fall back on. Teaching would give me summers off to play in tournaments and to practice.

Practice I did, but I didn't qualify for the tour. Instead, I qualified to teach elementary, middle, and high school. The Ladies Professional Golf Association rejected me, but the Ohio Department of Education accepted me. I did not travel around the country playing in tournaments on the LPGA Tour as I dreamed. The following stories are not about the victories and failures of a golf pro. They are 185 stories amassed from 30 years of victories and failures in the classroom.

My stories come from Madison, a small public school district in Ohio. The population is 50% white, 40% black, and 10% multiracial. Over 95% come from low income families and qualify for free or reduced lunch. With only about 670 students from K-12, one third the size of most schools, it would seem easy to keep the kids in line. Madison should run like a military academy. But if that were the case, I'd have no material of interest.

This is not a documentary, but a parody of the school system and a caricature of the people. In respect, the names have been changed. I wrote the stories to show what goes on inside a public school, as close as possible in the interest of reality.

Take the day I was talking to my 7th grade social studies class about civic issues. I used pot-hole repair as an example. Marvin woke up and looked around the room. He kept repeating *pot*. When he realized I wasn't passing any out, he went back to sleep. Or take the day I was leading my 6th graders back up to my room from the library. Josh got out of line and leaned against the railing, doubled over and out of breath. I told him I was 40 years older than he, but at least I could make it up the steps. "Man," he said, "I gotta quit smokin'."

I couldn't make this stuff up. How could I not write it down?

Meet me in Room 233 and I'll take you on a tour of a public school in Ohio, the only tour on which I ever competed.

185 DAYS

DAY 1
Honeymoon

My classroom has a clean carpet and the desks are in straight rows. I've been coming in for the past two weeks to get ready for the new school year. Papers are in neat stacks on my desk. The bulletin board above my desk reads: "Let every sluice of knowledge be open and set a flowing." John Adams's quote fills me with enthusiasm and optimism. The amendments are displayed above the dry erase board on the sidewall. The clock, the master of the school, separates the Bill of Rights from the rest of them. A poster of the presidents hangs on the back wall and pictures of Obama's Cabinet are on display above the computers. A basketball poster between the windows on the other side reads: "You'll always miss 100% of the shots you don't take."

Today begins my 25th year of teaching. No matter how many first days I've been through, I'm still anxious. I rehearse what I will do and say so the kids know who's in charge. The moment they enter the room, I'll assign them a seat of my choice, not theirs. I will go over the rules and syllabus with the class and require a parent signature. It's called covering your ass. If a student fails a quarter because he or she didn't turn in a notebook, there it is right in the syllabus that the complaining parent had signed, "Notebook: one-third of the grade." I'm ready.

But I know there's no such thing as ready. How does a teacher get ready for dysfunctional home lives, drugs, lack of sleep and proper nutrition, and, the worst of all, apathy?

There is a bustle in the hall as the kids enter the building. The laughter, pleasant banter among students and teachers, and general gladness to be back in school can only happen on the first morning. Rob Sands, last year's worst behavior problem, greets me as if I were his favorite rock star. "What's up, Ms. Ball? Did you hear the new song out by Korn?" He thinks I'm cool because I listen to hard rock and love Led Zeppelin. I notice he has added a few more face piercings over the summer. "Charming tongue and eyebrow," I remark. I remind myself that Rob is repeating my U.S. studies course since he failed all four quarters last year. I can't be too cool or I would have inspired him to pass the first time. How often will I kick him out of class this year for his incessant, off-topic gab?

The first bell class comes into my room. The kids give me my one big chance to thrill them. For a few minutes I'm someone different to look at. They're hoping I'll bring the pyrotechnics every day. Their heads are up and they listen as I go over the rules and syllabus. I'm almost fooled into believing they will comply. Perhaps they will arrive on time and be prepared with texts, notebooks, and pens. Perhaps they won't have brushes, lotion, makeup, and iPods. The honeymoon is over when I give out the first assignment: *Compare the political ideas of Montesquieu and Hobbes.* I am barraged with moans and complaints. So much for my ten minutes of fame.

It's hot out and I don't feel like working either. It's still summer after all. The kids will start working when the weather cools down, when it's not Friday or Monday, Halloween, the day before Thanksgiving and Christmas break, when they don't have the winter blahs, spring fever, or senioritis. The hell with it. There's no good day or time at school. This day is as good as any. I know it as I begin another year.

If it hadn't taken me 10 years to realize I wasn't good enough to play professional golf, this could be my last year. The bell rings and the kids move on to their next class. Another group comes in. My room has been christened: desks out of line, candy and gum wrappers on the floor, broken pencils, and forgotten notebooks and planners. Where's my caddy?

DAY 2
Names

The first week of school I look out at all the new faces in my largest class of 28 freshmen. *Who's going to give me grief this year?* Can't tell the first week. I am new to them too, and the honeymoon may last until Labor Day. To prepare for its end, I put students in assigned seats the moment they walk through the door. No one sits where they please. I deliver the message that this is my space and I'm in control.

I must learn their names as soon as possible to pinpoint and redirect a potential troublemaker. "Everybody, stand in front of the room. Lamuel (La-mule), first seat, first row."

"It's Lamuel (Lam-u-el)."

"Okay, sorry. Ambrea (Am-bree-a), behind Lamuel (La-mule)."

"It's Ambrea (Am-bray-a)." "It's Lamuel (Lam-u-el)."

"Okay, next: Tyren, James E., and James P. Second row: Tyrell, Breanna, Sydney, Hunter, and Demico. Once you get your seat, work on the current events questions I've placed on your desks. Tyrell, be quiet."

"I'm Tyren, don't you remember?"

"I'll remember your name soon enough if you keep talking. Third row: Barry, Ashley, D.J. O., D.J. W., Tariq, and Andrea (An-dree-a)."

"It's Andrea (An-dray-a)."

"Alright, Andrea (An-dray-a). Fourth row: Norma, Bre'Jon…"

"I have a hyphen not an apostrophe between the Bre and Jon."

"Glad to know that. Now, Joanie, Sabrina, Kiara (Ki-are-a), Austin."

"It's Kiara (Ki-air-a), Ms. Ball."

"Will you give me a few more days? I have 28 names to learn, and you only have one. And mine isn't very complicated." I write big angry letters on the board: B-A-L-L. "Fifth row: Se-von…"

"There's an apostrophe not a hyphen between the *Se* and *von*."

"As soon as I get Bre-Jon straight, I'll work on Se'von. Mary, after Se'von, then Tevin, Jake and Anthony. Tevin, quiet and answer your questions."

"I'm Tariq, Tevin just sat down."

"Tevin, Tyren, Tyrell, Tariq, I don't care. Quiet and do your work. I'll be calling your right name more than you'll ever want me to."

Two new students appear at my door with schedules. *You have got to be kidding.* These are the girls from Senegal who can't speak a word of English. They belong in kindergarten learning their ABCs, months, and days of the week. I never dreamed they'd be put in a 9th grade U.S. history class. "Welcome, Khardiatou (Kar-di-too), and Hawa (How-a)." They correct me.

"Khardiatou (Khar-di-a-too)." "Hawa (Ow-a)."

I motion them to desks beside Mary and Sydney, good ones to copy from. Then I take inventory of the class. Barry is autistic. Ashley and Joanie have 50 IQs. Four more of them are on IEPs. Casey has no fingers and I just got two ESL kids.

And I'm supposed to get them all to pass the social studies part of the Ohio Graduation Test by March—*Habeas Corpus, Plessy v. Ferguson, Brown v. Board of Education, The Cold War*. All these facts I must cram in their heads so Madison can earn its indicators for the school report card. I look past my class and out the window. It's 85 degrees and sunny. I could be playing golf right now. What made me return for my 26th year?

Breanna raises her hand. I'm heartened in anticipation of an insightful question about the current events I prepared during the summer. "Yes, Breanna."

"What time do we get out of here?"

"When the bell rings," I snap. I realize the OGT is making me irritable and I shouldn't take it out on the kids. I wish I could just teach to their abilities and love them and enjoy them without worrying about state test results. I soften a little. "Actually, Breanna, I've been wondering the same thing myself."

DAY 3
Connections

The people I love the best jump into work head first... Who strain
in the muck and the mud... who do what has to be done...
—Marge Percy

I have good old Bernice again this year. She is rather plump and wears
a different hair style and designer fingernails each day. One time she had
her hair in an absurd bell shape and provided the teachers with their
entertainment for the day. "I wish she'd spend one-tenth of the time on her
homework as she does on her grooming," I told another teacher who also has
her in class.

She agreed. "She just doesn't seem to make connections does she? Her
answers show no understanding of the concepts."

I had my U.S. studies class pretend they were delegates to the Second
Continental Congress. They had to write letters to the government of France
asking for help in fighting the British. Bernice's letter was abominable. I
couldn't read most of it, and what I could decipher made no sense. I told
her that her inch-long acrylic fingernails were getting in the way of her
penmanship, and that the Civil Rights Movement came almost two centuries
after the American Revolution. "Don't worry, Ms. Ball," she said good-
naturedly, "my nails have nothing to do with the way I write."

After this discussion, I was in front of the students intellectualizing about
how the ideas of the Enlightenment inspired both the American and French
Revolutions. The room was dark and the only sounds were the fan in the

overhead projector and my own voice. "The French Revolution turned even more violent during the Reign of Terror. Plato, one of our Enlightenment thinkers, warned that democracy too has its dangers." I was ending the lecture when I heard a rustling sound to my right. Kerri, a scraggly blonde, was standing over the garbage can removing the plastic liner.

"Where do you want me to put this, Ms. Ball, I just threw up." My stomach flipped. I guess I was too wrapped up in the Enlightenment to notice. The students sure did though. They were looking at me in anticipation. I took the bag from her and put it in the hall. The nurse's office was locked, so I told her to go to the main office and call her mom. "I'm okay," she said and went back to her seat. I guess she is, I considered. She can't be too sick if she thought of taking the liner out of the can. I started asking wrap up questions when Kerri got out of her seat, doubled over, and threw up again. Then she knelt down and started sobbing. Bernice went right to her, held her, and stroked her head. While I rummaged in the back of the room looking for a bag of Vo-Ban, the powder you throw on throw up, Bernice got a roll of paper towels and cleaned up the mess herself, fingernails and all.

Kerri fainted next. Did she need smelling salts, oxygen, CPR? I ran down the hall to unlock the nurse's office so we could at least get Kerri on a cot. When I entered what I thought was an empty room, I was infinitely relieved to see the nurse sitting in front of her computer. "I need help in my room. A student has vomited several times and has just fainted."

She looked at me as if I had intruded and took a bite of her apple. "I'm not on duty."

"A student is on the floor in my room and I don't know what to do," I said.

"What's the student's name?" she asked. I told her. "I don't have her paperwork."

I practically cried, "What does that have to do with an emergency?" She finally got up, took her blood pressure kit, and followed me to my room.

The nurse finally went to work once she saw Kerri on the floor. "Can you say your name? When did you eat last?" She went through Kerri's purse and took out two bottles of prescription medicine. "How many did you take? When did you take them last?" The nurse took her cell phone from her pocket and called the paramedics. They arrived, put Kerri on a stretcher and took her to the hospital. Her mother was instructed to supervise her medication.

The bell rang for lunch. I thanked Bernice for all of her help. "Oh, that ain't nothin, Ms. Ball. I'm used to taking care of people." I spent my lunch break getting the room back in order, wondering who wasn't making connections. Bernice surpassed two professionally trained adults, stroking Kerri's head, making a pillow out of her jacket, and cleaning the throw up with a roll of paper towels. I, on the other hand, fumbled for a bag of Vo-Ban and the nurse took a bite of her apple.

DAY 4
School Lunches

Salami, baloney, mustard and cheese,
Whatever I pack it just doesn't please.

It sits in brown paper all morning long,
When I take the first bite I know something's wrong.

Peanut butter and jelly, that insipid taste,
I'll crumble it with the foil and put it to waste.

Ham and mayo soggy and sleazy,
Just to smell it makes me queasy.

White bread, rye, marble or wheat,
After five hours it's no good to eat.

Carrot sticks, apples, raisins, and chips,
When I see those in baggies my stomach flips.

Wendy's, Panera where are you I pray?
Never in school at midday.

DAY 5
Heads or Tails

It's a coin toss going into school each day. I don't know which side of my students will show up. Will it be a heads day? Will they use their brains and demonstrate higher order thinking? Or will it be a tails day? Will they act like butts, asses, and low functioning species? More importantly, will it be a heads or tails day for me? Will I be proactive and think before I speak? Or will I react to every disturbance and entertain the kids with my tirades? Many nights I have lain in bed reviewing my day. Devastated, I realize how I could have decelerated instead of accelerated bad behavior.

One time during a writing assignment, my student My'easha called out, "This is boring, I ain't doin' this."

My tail snapped at her. "Every second of your life can't be electrifying. Make your choice, do it or take a zero." I should have paused, grinned at her and said, "You love it, you know it. Need an idea to get started?" Why didn't I respond with my head?

I was a tail when Kim wouldn't take her scarf off because her hair was messed up. "You can't wear scarves in the classroom. Take it off or I'm writing you a detention." Why didn't I say, "Kim, please take your scarf off. You're so cute your hair won't matter."

How hard can it be to lightly turn an attitude and dispel animosity? It can be very hard some days because I'm no different from the kids. I'm human and have a tail as well as a head.

DAY 6
Heads

Today I gave my language arts students an assignment in the form of a journal entry. They had to write about a real or imaginary experience, recalling the sights, sounds, smells, thoughts and feelings connected with the event. I did the assignment right along with them. After the entries were written, I asked each student to read his journal aloud while the others jotted down read back lines. Then we took turns naming the writer and repeating his words.

Brooke: We are on our way to Alie's dad's ex-girlfriend's house.

Tyler: I was hoping for a Playstation 2.

Ben: I heard part of a conversation about backpacks.

Alison: The boys and girls club would pick you up in a limousine to go to the restaurant.

Jessica: The air smelled like fresh flowers.

Jeremiah: In Canada I had $50 and they gave me $100.

Shayla: Candy was delivering puppies on some ripped up pieces of newspaper.

Heather: I thought that she would not like my gift.

Mrs. Ball: I banged my golf club into the ground and sucked a blister on my finger.

Shayla: We could still smell the chili my aunt was cooking.

Jessica: I told my mom I would not leave until she got me that kitten.

Rodney: I can ramp walls, grind curbs, and even jump gaps.

Today was a heads day. The students were absorbed in their writing, and I was complacent in my ability to lead the class and get the best out of each student.

DAY 7
Tails

Today the coin fell on tails. It was 8:45 and time to pick up my class from the library. The librarian looked haggard. "Mrs. Ball, we didn't have a good class this morning. Some students refused to stand for the Pledge of Allegiance, wasted their research time, argued with each other, and disrespected me."

Anger rushed through me. "I'm sorry, Mrs. Wright. I'll take care of it."

"The students don't realize how lucky they are to have these resources available to them," continued Mrs. Wright. "Look at our 20 up-to-date computers, all the books, and the brand new tables, chairs and carpet in this room. Mrs. Chatterjee and I have been working all summer preparing the library for the boys and girls." She was usually so soft spoken, calm, and patient with the kids. But today her voice cracked in agitation.

"I've lectured them about this repeatedly, Mrs. Wright. They are the luckiest children in the world to be born in the United States and receive a free education. Our democracy allows them to choose their careers and work to advance their own lives. If they were born in a Third World country, they'd be working in a factory making products that American children get to enjoy. They'd earn enough each day just so their families could eat."

"I'd like some of you in here to switch places with a 13-year-old child in Indonesia for a week," said Mrs. Wright. "Maybe then you would respect this school and the opportunities all around you in this country."

Robert was making faces, demonstrating he was neither respectful nor grateful, attracting the attention of other students. I yelled, "Get out of this library. You don't deserve to be in here. You can sit in the hall for the next two hours and make faces at the walls. Anyone else who shows one speck of an attitude today will join Robert. Now line up."

I apologized again to Mrs. Wright as I led my class out of the library. On the way up to my classroom, I made several stops to check on hallway behavior. I dropped Robert off at a desk outside of my room as the rest went inside.

The kids sat down and I went to the board to begin our spelling contest. Rodney mocked me as I explained the rules. "Out," I snapped. I directed Rodney to another spot in the hall and slammed the door.

All during the contest I was in a state of panic. Kids aren't supposed to be in the hallways unsupervised. The assistant principal wasn't in his office and I had nowhere else to send them. I backed myself into a corner. *What if they wander out of the building? What if they get hurt? What if I get a lawsuit? What if I get fired?* But I couldn't let Rodney back into the room or let Robert know I was the least bit concerned about him. And I didn't want to lose my credibility with the rest of the class. Several others were on the edge of defiance. Any weakness shown by me would cause chaos. *Never let them see you sweat.*

Just then the door opened and Rodney slinked across the front of the room and headed for his desk. "You don't come into this room unless I say so," I shouted.

"I just did, didn't I?"

"Yes, and you're going right back out."

"Man, I'm getting something out of my desk."

I stood in front of it. "You won't need anything in there for the hall." He kept walking toward it, but I walked toward him and backed him out of the room. All the while he was mocking me and degrading the school.

I finished the contest and got the students settled into some seatwork. I rushed to my laptop and sent my team teacher across the hall an email. *Please check on Robert and Rodney for me. I threw them out of class and I can't let anyone know I'm worried.* Afraid she wouldn't check her email soon enough, I called her room. "It's me," I whispered. "Check your email."

She replied within a few minutes. *Robert has his head down on the desk. Rodney was walking all over the hall. I tried to reason with him but he kept talking back. I told him I wasn't dealing with him and sent him to the office with a referral.*

A half hour later, the principal, Mrs. Brown, called my room. "Send some work to me for Rodney. He'll spend the rest of the day in the second grade because that's how he's behaving."

Yes! I said to myself, infinitely relieved and grateful to Mrs. Brown. I went out to get Robert since his designated two hours had elapsed. "Would you like to be admitted into the room for social studies?" He nodded and seemed humble enough, so I let him back in. Victorious over my students, I felt great.

Driving home after school, though, I knew I wasn't great and my victory was only temporary. I could look forward to a night of thrashing in bed, remorsefully rewriting my script from tails to heads.

DAY 8
Something to Hide

This year our school adopted a new dress code. Students have to wear a plain collared shirt tucked in and khaki pants with a belt. Our principal reprimanded the teachers during a faculty meeting for not helping the administration enforce the dress code. Determined to do my part, I told Lori, the first one to come into my room in violation, to tuck her shirt in. Her face turned red and she said, "I can't." When I insisted, she ran to the bathroom sobbing hysterically. Stephanie ran after her then reported back to me. "Mrs. Ball, she's pregnant," Stephanie whispered. Of course all the kids knew it, and for the rest of the class there was the undercurrent of *Mrs. Ball is a bitch*. "I'm sorry," I told Lori later, "I had no idea. You're so quiet and little, I didn't notice." Since that incident, I treat shirt tucking gingerly. Rules aren't as black and white and easy to enforce as they appear in the student handbook.

DAY 9
Tiger Mom

Theresa Collins, a mother of one of my students, has her solution to teenage pregnancy. "Babies are made between 3 p.m. and 6 p.m. when parents are at work," she said. "My sons ain't makin' no babies. I pick them up from school at 3:00 and take them back to work with me until I get off. We all go home together, eat dinner together, do homework, and go to bed—alone."

DAY 10
Earning Respect

    Wesley is a 9ᵗʰ grader with glasses, buckteeth, and a 140 IQ. I was passing back Enlightenment essays, and Jake, a 12ᵗʰ grader repeating the class, noticed that Wesley got a 50%. What Wesley wrote was outstanding, but he only did half of the assignment. "Wow, Wesley got an F!" said Jake breaking into a satisfied grin showing his chipped front tooth. He turned his head of stringy, shoulder length hair to Wesley and said, "I have newfound respect for you today."

DAY 11
Rhetoric Meets Reality

I made sure that my students got to watch Obama's back to school address to the nation on the Tuesday after Labor Day. At noon, broadcast time, I had my biggest and worst world history class, 22 boys and only 3 girls. Maybe Obama could enlighten them. "Quiet, everyone," I yelled as I turned on the TV, turned off the lights, and shut the door.

We looked up at the screen. The atmosphere at Wakefield High in Virginia was electric. Crisply attired Arne Duncan, the Secretary of Education, gave a smooth introduction. Then Wakefield's poised valedictorian spoke. The captivated student body and staff awaited the president.

Twenty-five ninth graders were packed into my classroom, designed to hold no more than 18 desks. It got stuffy a few minutes into the program. The boys had been to gym in the morning and had just come from lunch. I couldn't open the windows because of the noise from I-75; and I had to keep the door shut to muffle the racket the middle school kids were making in the hallway. *"And we've got students tuning in from all across America…"* Obama was saying. Yes we do, I thought, fresh from gym and lunch, with BO and smelly farts. The cafeteria food was starting to kick in. The kids were covering their noses with their shirts and murmuring accusations at one another.

"Quiet," I scolded walking up and down the rows, "the president is speaking!"

"Pay attention… put in the hard work," he was saying.

"Get your head off the desk," I whispered to Tony. I prodded him several times but he wouldn't wake up.

"And that's what I want to focus on today: the responsibility each of you has for your education."

I gave up on Tony and walked over to Maurice. He was focused on a miniature skateboard rolling down his desk. I took it away from him. His head stunk like it hadn't been washed in two weeks. *"I know a lot of you have challenges in your lives right now that can make it hard to focus on your schoolwork."* I wondered what Maurice's challenges were to cause him to come to school smelling of neglect.

"I hope you'll all wash your hands a lot … so we can keep people from getting the flu this fall and winter." Da'von let out a ferocious wet sneeze. There was no escaping it no matter how many times we washed our hands.

I rushed over to Dylan and DJ to quiet their laughing. They were poking each other in the stomach with their pencils. *"So I expect you to get serious this year,"* concluded Obama. *"I expect you to put your best effort into everything you do."*

I turned on the lights and faced my audience. I wished Obama could come to my room to see where his rhetoric meets reality. Opening the windows was the only meaningful thing I could do. I raised my voice over I-75. "Tomorrow we'll discuss the president's speech and then continue our notes on the Enlightenment."

DAY 12
Follow Up

"What was the message your president wanted to give you in his speech yesterday?" I asked the class first thing the next day. Tommy kicked Barry's desk out of line. "Tommy, keep your feet in your own area."

"It wasn't me," he whined pointing to Barry. "He keeps messin' with me."

Greg raised his hand. "President Obama told us we should stay in school, work hard, and take responsibility for our own actions."

"Exactly. Tommy, did you hear what Greg just said? Greg, go write that on the board."

Greg wrote the messages big in three different colors. "Great," I said. "We'll leave those on display all during our study of the Enlightenment Era. It looks like we're ready to begin."

DAY 13
Laying the Foundation

Since 9/11, I have always tried to give my history students background information on this world changing event. "The terrorists didn't just wake up one day and decide to fly airplanes into the World Trade Center and the Pentagon," I explain. I pull down the wall-sized world map and point to the Middle East. I talk about the Arabs and the Jews who have been fighting over the same land for centuries, the United States' support of Israel, the sacredness of this region for the religions of Islam, Judaism, and Christianity, and how oil plays a big part in our involvement in the Middle East.

Today, Michael was staring intently at the map. I had my heart set on an insightful question when he raised his hand. "Why do they call Turkey, Turkey? Is it because of Thanksgiving or something?" I was totally lost until David got up and pointed to the country just north of the site of the Middle East crisis. *Oh, well,* I thought, *at least I have them looking in the general vicinity anyway.*

DAY 14
Growth but not Grown

"That's racist," laughed Dion with his stock comment for everything. He was looking at one of the many news articles I taped on the board for our summer current events lesson. Students were circulating around the room obtaining information from the articles. Dion kept laughing and pointing at the picture of Kim Phuc, the eight-year-old girl who ran naked and screaming from her Vietnam village after a napalm attack.

"I didn't choose that article to entertain you, Dion," I said. "It's one of the most widely recognized and tragic photos of the Vietnam War. And racist is not an umbrella word for every situation." When the timer went off, the kids sat down and our discussion began. "Fred, read the first question."

"What happened to Kim Phuc on June 8, 1972?" He read in a fake academic voice twice as slowly as necessary.

"Fred, please read normally," I said.

"Yeah, Fred," interrupted Se'Von, "read the question properly."

"Se'Von," I said, "I'll do the correcting."

"She was the victim of a napalm attack on her village," said Fred exaggerating a normal voice.

"I chose that article because this summer was the 40th anniversary of…"

"That's racist," blurted Dion.

"Dion," I said, "don't cut me off. And I've already told you the Pulitzer Prize-winning photo is neither racist nor funny."

Sarah raised her hand. "I read that now she travels the world as a peace activist."

"Thanks, Sarah. At the beginning of her adulthood she hid from the media then she decided…"

"to come out of the closet," blurted Dion again.

"That's gay," added Se'Von.

"No, that's racist," interjected Fred.

I glared at the three boys. Who should I strangle first? "She decided to turn her tragedy into something positive." I was totally exasperated and we had 34 more questions to go. "Do you think I or any student in here could finish a sentence without getting cut off? A meaningful discussion is impossible because three people are constantly interrupting."

"Yeah, and we all happen to be black," announced Dion.

He was pushing my buttons but I couldn't stop. "Race has nothing to do with this. The Civil Rights Movement ended 50 years ago. This is the 21st century. When I stand in front of the class, I don't see black or white. I see good behavior or bad behavior."

"All I said was me, Fred, and Se'Von are black," said Dion.

"That didn't occur to me," I said wondering why I was arguing with him.

Fred, overflowing his desk at 300 pounds, kicked Se'Von's desk and threw the whole row out of line. "Fred," I shouted.

"You ain't see what Se'Von just did?" Dion was laughing and egging the two on.

"I see three seniors in the honors government class acting like third graders. I have no problem kicking you all out. If I were you I'd be embarrassed sitting in the office with the freshmen. You'd think by now you'd be tired of detentions, suspensions, and Saturday schools." I've taught Dion, Se'Von, and Fred since their freshman year and the only growth they've demonstrated is physical. "Now shut up and grow up so we can continue. If you're so interested in race, I have some real questions on the topic further down, if you're still in the room when we get there."

DAY 15
In Her Absence

As I headed to the front of the room to start class, Megan trapped me behind my desk. "Did we *do anything* yesterday? I wasn't here."

"No, Megan, I cancelled my lesson and we sat in silence with our hands folded for fifty minutes in honor of your absence. Of course we *did something*. And to avoid my sarcasm next time, try asking me what work you need to make up instead of if we *did anything*. Now go sit down and see me after class."

DAY 16
In His Presence

"Ms. Ball, you ain't never absent," said Se'Von, noticing my cough. "And you always make us work. Why don't you take a day off so we can have a sub."

"I don't like taking off," I replied. "It's more work preparing for a sub than just coming to work."

"Well, just don't give us nothin' to do when you're out."

"Why don't you focus on your work instead of my attendance," I said. "Besides, how do you think I feel? I see your name on the absence list, and just when I think I'm going to get a break, you roll in late, just in time for my class."

DAY 17
Over Qualified

During a faculty meeting, teachers brought up the problem of kids coming to school high, smelling of alcohol, cigarettes, or marijuana. Mrs. Gordon, who has seniors for homeroom, offered her solution. "First thing," she said, "I do a homeroom sweep. As soon as I smell something on a student, I send him or her to Dr. McCoy."

"Mrs. Gordon is right," nodded Dr. McCoy, our assistant principal in charge of discipline. "If you suspect any form of substance abuse, just send them to me," he said. "The only way to detect it initially is to do a smell check." He shook his head and gestured to the faculty, his neck squeezed in his collar and tie, flesh shaking on his cheeks like a bulldog. "I went back to school and got my doctorate only to smell kids' breath."

We all laughed sympathetically. "You have me beat," I announced. "I buy Kleenex with my own money and set it on the window sill for everyone. Students yank it out, blow their noses, then throw their dirty tissues on the floor. When I ask them to use the garbage can, they refuse and walk out of the room. I have two master's degrees only to pick up dirty Kleenex after kids. But I don't have a PhD and I don't have to smell kids' breath."

Dr. McCoy nodded appreciatively and the faculty clapped for the hard working man who always backs his teachers.

DAY 18
Nothing to Write With

It took me several weeks to snap. I've been giving my homeroom students Bic pens since the beginning of school. Every morning four or five seniors ask me for something to write with. Every morning I break open my ten pack that I buy with my own money and dole them out. This morning 6'3" Oumar approached my desk. As athletes are required on game days, he was dressed up for Friday night basketball. "Ms. Ball, do you have a pencil?"

I usually feel sorry for the scruffy kids, suck it up, and toss them a pen. But for some reason Oumar's appearance unnerved me. "Look at you," I snapped. "You're all duded out in your vest, tie, jacket, nice shoes, and big red ear phones; and you don't even care enough to bring a pencil to class. I'm sick to death of it."

In shock, Oumar went to the board and took a dry erase marker from the ledge. "Don't even think of using that for my work," I scolded. In more shock, Oumar sat down and asked around for a writing utensil. Justin dug deep in his pocket. Several minutes later Oumar held half of a chewed up pencil with not nearly enough lead to complete his assignment. "Are you going to play with a deflated ball tonight?" I asked touching the jagged end of Justin's gift.

"No, Ma'am," he said.

"You might as well," I said. "If you don't start bringing a pencil to class, you won't be eligible for the next game."

DAY 19
Nothing to Write On

Ronnie never brings paper, notebook, text, or homework to class. His attendance is pretty good and I can't figure out what he's thinking by coming to school and still failing. Today kids were taking notes on the Spanish American War. "Teddy Roosevelt and his Rough Riders captured San Juan Hill," I was saying when Ronnie got up, sauntered to the pencil sharpener, talking and tugging at his baggy pants along the way. He took a brand new No. 2 from his ear and turned the noisy crank infinitely longer than necessary. "Sit down," I yelled. "What do you need a pencil for?" All eyes went from Ronnie's ghost white face to his empty desk. Figuring he didn't have an argument, he sat back down.

DAY 20
Dress Code

"Tuck in your shirt," I told Zach today. Five minutes later it was hanging out.

"Take your hoodie off, Jamie." Five minutes later she put it back on.

"Pull up your pants," I yelled to Miles and Dawaun. "You walk like you have a load." Five minutes later their pants were down below their butts again.

Teachers are expected to be teachers, counselors, nurses, and disciplinarians. Now we're supposed to dress the 150 students who come through our classrooms each day. A school uniform policy is the latest innovation adopted by many public schools over the last several years. It's supposed to make the kids work and behave better, and eliminate the three Bs: boobs, butts, and bellies. The only change I've noticed is that it is one added strain on a teacher's time and energy and one more diversion for the students.

Both boys and girls are required to wear khaki pants with a belt, and a solid polo shirt tucked in. Sandals and hoodies are not allowed. That sounds simple and easy to enforce. But the combinations, modifications, and ways of getting around this code show that the kids really are capable of higher order thinking. For example, girls wear foot wide glitzy belts, lacy camisoles under their unbuttoned polos, and Three Musketeer boots over their slacks. Boys wear long-sleeved t-shirts under their polos and wild striped socks that they show off by rolling up their pants. Too bad Madison doesn't offer a course in fashion design.

Every day is like the first day of school even though this is the fourth year of our uniform policy. Every day, every class, every hour I start all over with the same boring exchange with the same students.

"Take your hoodie off, Jamie."

"I'm cold."

"Then bring a jacket without a hood."

"I don't have one."

"If you're cold enough you'll come up with one."

"I can't afford it."

"I see you have a BlackBerry and an iPod. You can certainly afford a $15 jacket from Target."

I turn to Zach. "Tuck in your shirt."

"You don't say nothin' to the girls. Look at Sarah."

"Your shirt is down below your knees. Sarah's is at her hip. I'm correcting the worst eyesores first."

Zach continues to argue. "That ain't fair."

"Guess what happened to me this morning," I said. "I got a speeding ticket and wasn't the only one speeding. The cop couldn't stop everyone at once." That made half sense to him. He tucked the front in and walked away from me with the back hanging out.

I get so tired of saying, "Tuck your shirt in," that sometimes I say, "*Put* your shirt in," hoping to get a different result.

"You don't have yours tucked in," they say.

"I'm so flattered you think I look young enough to be a student. I wore a uniform for thirteen years. It wasn't nearly as comfortable and stylish as yours. We had to wear plaid pleated skirts, white blouses, green blazers with nametags on the lapel, bobby socks, and saddle oxfords. In the winter our legs froze going to and from school. Khaki pants, a polo shirt, a fleece, and gym shoes would have been a luxury beyond our comprehension."

My testimony stopped the argument for a while until Cooper entered my room without a belt. "Go to Mrs. Barrett's room and get a belt."

"You don't have one on."

"I'm so flattered you think I look young enough to be a student."

Yesterday the principal, Mr. Howard, was standing by my door when the bell rang. A student came out with a dress code violation and I got reprimanded instead of the student. The principal, I thought, needed a lesson on visibility. He should be circulating daily throughout the school and enforcing the rules instead of sitting in his office reading the sports page and talking with the coaches. Nevertheless, I made a stronger effort that afternoon. I told April to tuck in her shirt. She turned red and headed to the restroom. The kids informed me that she was pregnant. They acted as though I had committed a crime.

That incident reinforced my dislike of making personal comments to students. I especially hate telling heavyset girls, and now pregnant ones, to tuck in when they are trying to hide under an XL polo. Then there's always the question of judgment. When a kid is out of uniform but is sitting quietly and no one else seems to notice, should I stop my lesson and correct him, risking a confrontation or even a temper tantrum? Is it worth it to disrupt rare moments when most of the class is engaged in the work?

The only leverage I have is when kids come to me for favors. *Can I go to the nurse? Can I get a drink? Will you write me a letter of recommendation? Can I leave my gym bag in your room till after school?*

Not with your hoodie on. Not with your shirt out. That seems to get their attention and they scramble to arrange their clothes. When they get what they want it's back to the tiresome exchange. "Tuck your shirt in."

"You never say nothin' to Justin."

"When I take care of you, I'll get someone else. A cop can't stop everyone at once for speeding."

"Zach, please tuck your shirt in, Mr. Howard is coming to observe me."

"You don't have yours tucked in."

"I'm so flattered you think I look young enough to be a student…"

DAY 21
The Last Word

"You're five minutes late," I said to Adam when he ambled into my class.

"I was taking a five minute poop," he smarted back to me. The class roared in appreciation.

I handed him a detention. "Then you need to start it five minutes earlier next time," I retorted.

DAY 22
Direct Discourse

"I wish I was in Mr. Hoff's history class," said Ecila. "It's so fun. He don't make us do no work."

"Yeah, this class is so boring," stated Nikky. She looked at the clock. "Oh my God, there's still a half-hour till lunch." She put her head on the desk and covered it with her jacket.

"Thanks for the feedback, girls," I said. "You do wonders for my self-esteem."

DAY 23
Instant Imperialism

Nicole has not made it to school for a five day week since the start of the year. She averages two to three days a week at best. She had just returned from a run of eight straight days out. I had just taught a unit on imperialism and was about to give a test.

"What's imperialism?" she asked, all put out as I distributed the tests.

"Nicole," I said, "I can't stop class now and teach you eight days of work in one minute. Read chapter nine, and then see me after class."

"Well, you don't have to get an attitude," she said. "She's so mean," she told her friends jerking open her book. They buzzed in agreement not wanting to take the test any more than she.

DAY 24
Study? Hell!

I noticed a new student in the hall this morning with bleached blonde hair, tight jeans, and a short black leather jacket. Sure enough she showed up in my afternoon study hall and handed me her schedule. I checked it to confirm she was in the right room at the right time. "Welcome to Madison," I said.

She rolled her eyes while I explained that during study hall the students sit in assigned seats, keep quiet, and bring something to work on every day.

"You must be trippin'," she said. "You need to chill out. You must have issues."

"You're pretty brave for your first day," I said showing her to her seat and handing her the rules. "If you can't follow these, you'll be the one with issues."

DAY 25
The Freshmen

It seems the kids are getting worse every year, unless I'm getting older, out of touch, and out of energy. This year's freshmen are from hell. It's going to take me all quarter to train them. What did they do last year? Mr. Parks, their 8th grade teacher, must have let them run wild. It doesn't help that I have them at the end of the day when my nerves are shot along with their ability to focus.

I had my first major run in with five of the girls. They all had the same wording to answers on my Declaration of Independence quiz. *King George III is the so called He*, they wrote to the question, *To whom does the long list of grievances refer?*

"It's somewhere in the book like that," said De'Asha.

"No it's not," I replied, "I've read that chapter ten times. And how come you all chose the same five signers of the Declaration out of 57 choices?

"We ain't cheat," said Ashley.

"One of you did the work, and the rest of you copied. You all have Fs. If you want to change your grade come after school and take the quiz over."

They left the room exclaiming, "I ain't cheat!" "I'm tellin my mamma on her!" "That ain't fair!" "She lyin!"

The whole class is so noisy I can't talk, teach, or give simple directions. I spent two hours one Saturday making up a game thinking I could trick them into learning. On Monday I put the kids in a circle, an ordeal in itself, and gave each kid a card. On one side was a term and on the other side the definition of someone else's term. Adam started with *Thomas Jefferson* and someone was to respond *author of the Declaration of Independence*, then read out his term. The goal is to match all the terms in less than five minutes. After several attempts and lots of chaos, I gave up. "Everybody, sit down!" I yelled.

Desperate, I assigned vocabulary. "Look these words up in the glossary and write the definitions in your notebook. What you don't finish will be for homework." I had to give low level seat work to quiet everyone down and to give myself a reprieve.

The next day I walked by each desk and checked that easy assignment. I was appalled to find that only six kids out of 26 had completed the eight definitions. *I'll show them,* I thought. I gave a new assignment and said, "Don't be surprised if you have a test on this tomorrow." The next day I gave a test and when they handed it in I gave them more work for a grade. I kept them so busy no one had time to talk. Except for Margaret, that is, who went to the back of the room to talk to Erica.

"Margaret, sit down," I said.

"I was just asking her a question," she sassed in her raspy voice.

"Erica's not teaching the class."

"Oh my God, chill out," she said.

"I have no intention of chilling out, and don't give me orders." The patience I'd given her since Day 1 had expired. "Go to the office." I can deal with my 18-year-old thugs in government more easily than this 80 pound blonde wisp.

"You're so lame," she announced crumbling her paper and storming out of the room.

I was more dumbfounded that such a weathered voice could come from a 14-year-old than I was by her disrespect. She sounds like a 60-year-old chain smoker.

After I quieted the ruckus from Margaret's scene, I noticed my book was missing from my desk. I checked the closest row and discovered that Ci Ci had it. "Where's your book?" I asked.

"This is mine," she said.

I pointed to my name on the inside cover. "Your book should have your name and number here."

"Oh, well this was in my locker. Someone must have switched with me."

"I just used this book before class. It couldn't have been in your locker. Don't remove anything from my desk and don't lie to me."

Just then, Chasity came into the room wearing a hoodie. "I'm in ISS, I need my work," she said.

"I only give work to students who follow the dress code."

"Mr. Gentry lets us wear them," she said.

"You won't in here," I snapped feeling no need to be nice to anyone serving In-School Suspension. "Now get out and figure out what you have to do to get the assignment." The hoodie must have been more important than the work, for she never returned.

Slowly, I'm training them to do things my way. This year there will be no cheating, lying, talking out, or stealing. They must bring their own books, notebooks, and homework to class wearing no hoodies, and with shirts tucked in.

Today at the end of class I was asking review questions and remembered I had some Jolly Ranchers in my desk. So for each correct answer I gave one out. I was embarrassed because they were sticking together. They were from last year and had been sitting in my desk all summer. "They're stale," I apologized. "Do you still want them?" Justin got the next question right. His eyes got big and he gladly accepted the old candy from my bag. So did Adam and Jessica after him. When the bell rang I set the Jolly Ranchers on an empty desk and the kids sprang towards them as though they were starving. They grabbed and pushed to get at every last one. Kids that desperate for a treat, I thought, can't be all bad. "Tomorrow I'll bring in a fresh bag if you like them that much," I said. Maybe I'm starting to warm up to them.

DAY 26
Pot

"A civic issue is any issue that involves the public," I stated to my social studies class. "Examples of civic issues are recycling, garbage collection, building a stadium, and pot-hole repair."

Marvin woke up and looked around the room. "Ms. Ball said *pot*." He looked at me. "Did you say *pot?*" He looked around the room again. "Ms. Ball said *pot!*"

"Not that kind of pot, Marvin," I said. "Go back to sleep."

DAY 27
Lawsuit

"I'm going to sue you," Austin said to me when I handed him his third office referral."

"Go ahead," I said. "Teachers don't make any money."

DAY 28
Doggin' It

Saturday morning in the beauty parlor, waiting for the dye to take on my hair, I picked up a magazine. It was a publication I'd never heard of called *Marie Claire*. Absently, I turned the pages until the title of an article stopped me, "Kids Tolerate Mom's Hobby." I read that Mom's hobby was to go dogging, a practice popular in the United Kingdom. With a partner she goes out and has sex in public. According to the show they put on, the exhibitionists can attract new partners. People get pleasure out of watching and being watched. "I feel powerful knowing others want me," quoted the mother. *Christ*, I thought, *who has time for such excesses?* The closest I ever came to "going dogging" was at school yesterday.

At 12:50 Friday afternoon, I was "doggin' it" alright. A few minutes remained in fifth bell and I wondered how I would make it through the sixth and seventh. My excesses of the week included a 13-hour school day on Tuesday with Open House until 8:30, a Wednesday afternoon and evening devotion to my mom—bath, dinner, laundry, and grocery shopping, and on Thursday, a pile of papers to grade until 10 p.m.

A wave of ennui swept through me as I thought of the upcoming class. I had the low group for Ohio Graduation Test preparation. The students were unruly and hard to motivate and I had a tedious lesson to teach. On top of it I looked crappy. My baggy khaki slacks and faded olive green polo shirt were as dull as my energy, and my hair frizzed out of shape from the damp weather. *Just take it five minutes at a time, lay low, and the school day is bound to be over eventually,* I figured.

Just as I braced myself for the worst 50 minutes of the day, the secretary informed me I would have a parent visitor in my class. Of all times to be on display. I felt horrible, looked horrible, and had a horrible lesson to teach. *Be flexible*, I thought. I could do my cool power point presentation on the Constitution. The colorful flashing images would focus everyone's attention on the screen and off of me. *Damn it*, I wasn't signed up for the projector.

There was no more time to think as the class scattered into the room. I greeted the parent who told me to call him Steve and sat him next to his daughter. I felt like a goon as I read questions from the board on the Spanish American War and pointed out page numbers in the text for answers.

The regulars began their act calling across the room to each other.

"Your Mama ugly."

"Don't you go talkin' 'bout my Mama."

"Shut up."

"No, you shut up."

"My'easha and Robert go to the office," I commanded, as my shaking hands fumbled in the desk drawer for a referral form. *What does this parent think of me*, I wondered. *Can't she manage a class any better than this?*

I pointed to the next question on the board. Miraculously the class settled down and I noticed Steve eagerly looking up answers with his daughter. When he raised his hand I called him Larry. I could have killed myself. Here is this parent interested enough to come to school and check on his daughter, and I call him the wrong name. When he read his answer from the text, he couldn't pronounce some of the words. *Maybe he doesn't know a good lesson from a bad lesson*, I hoped as the class mercifully ended.

"Thank you for visiting," I said to Steve, feeling like a total flop. Although he was pleasant and supportive, I knew I didn't put on a good show and didn't enjoy being seen by anyone "doggin' it." No, I wasn't engaging in flamboyant public sex, but was hanging out there in the classroom fully exposed.

DAY 29
Ps and Cs

Today in senior government we discussed a section from the book about political campaigns. Then I showed a short video on primaries and caucuses. Devon had his head down at first but came to life after the video.

"Number the next page of your notebooks from one to ten," I said. "We're having a mini quiz on what we just saw. First question: Why are the Iowa and New Hampshire primaries so important? Devon, turn around and stop talking."

He ignored me and turned back to Tim. "Primaries and caucuses, penises and cocks," he snickered.

I stopped class and glared at him. "That is what a 5th grader would find amusing," I said. Devon turned red and sober and shrunk back into his desk.

DAY 30
Stink Bombs

This morning fourth period, my bell from hell, started out with the usual disruptions. "I like your sweater, Ms. Ball," Jody called out right in the middle of my notes on the French Revolution.

"She has about five like that in different colors," Lynn informed the class.

"How many kids do you have?" said Jody.

"Are you married?" asked Lynn. They were taunting me.

"You don't need to know that to pass world studies."

I gave more notes then stopped to show a clip from the new movie, *Marie Antoinette*. "I want you to pay special attention to Versailles and how the nobility lived in luxury, while 98% of the peasants didn't even have enough to eat." I fumbled with the DVD. "Look what she's doing," announced Lynn. "She's trying to lift it from the sides."

"She can't even get a DVD out of the case," squealed Jordan in delight. The two girls went back and fourth talking about me as though I weren't there. "You press the middle and it pops up, Ms. BALLS."

I did that and the whole class laughed. Excuse me, I wanted to scream, my husband is being treated for cancer and my mother is an invalid. I don't get to sit around and watch movies every night.

While I was fast-forwarding to the dining hall scene, Dashawn, another choice student, blurted out, "You coming to our game tomorrow night, Ms. Ball? How come you never come to our games?" I almost told him, if your performance on the field is no better than what it is in class, I see no reason to waste my time.

I found the right spot in the movie, and just when I thought I had it made, Matt, a 6'8", 280 pound football player got out of his seat and threw something against the wall. It made a fizzing sound. Jody screamed, "Ew, somebody farted!" She put her hand on her nose, and ran to the window. The whole room stunk.

I confronted Matt. "I saw you throw something."

"It was only a pencil."

"Why would you throw a pencil against the wall?" Matt shrugged and I let it go. It all happened so fast; I wasn't sure what just went on.

Patric stood in the hall wheezing and coughing. "This bothers my asthma," he said with his shirt over his face. I sent him to the nurse, opened the windows, and sprayed air freshener around the room.

I got everyone back in their seats and played just a fraction of what I intended of the movie before the bell ended. "Tomorrow we'll discuss the causes of the French Revolution in light of the palace of Versailles."

At the beginning of the next bell, Mr. Howard, the principal and football coach, made an announcement over the intercom. "If anyone has any information on who has been throwing stink bombs around the school, please come to the office. I intend to get to the bottom of this, and when I find out who the students are, they will be expelled." Yes, I thought. So that's what that smell was. Validated, I wrote Matt up on a referral form and took it to Mr. Howard.

The next day, Matt was back in my classroom, wearing his football jersey no less. After class I went into Mr. Howard's office. "I thought you said the students with the stink bombs would be expelled. I lost forty minutes of instruction yesterday because of Matt, and Patric had an asthma attack. Wasn't my word good enough?"

"Well," he hedged, "we needed to nail them all. One was thrown in the basement too during fourth period. I'm suspending Matt for three days."

I went back to my room fuming. If it were some puny kid who didn't play football, he'd be gone. But he needed Matt for his team for the rest of the season, especially the playoffs. Now that really stinks.

DAY 31
Back it Up

The writing portion of the state test was coming up in a few days. I was pretty intense as I gave my class some tips to sharpen their responses. I wanted to do a good job so the kids would be successful and the superintendent would be happy with me and their scores.

"If you say that a character acts independently, back it up with a fact, quote, or example from the reading. You could add, *Daniel raised his hand without looking around to see how the others were voting*. Always write something specific to impress the person scoring your paper."

Satisfied with my lesson, I looked at the class. "Does anyone have any comments? Jake?"

"Mrs. Ball, you look constipated."

The class fell silent waiting to see how I'd respond.

"Well," I gulped, "Back it up."

DAY 32

No Merit in Merit Pay

The Obama Administration, state legislators, and other education "experts" are touting merit pay for teachers as a way of improving our failing schools. Just what constitutes merit and on what will it be based? Do they understand the day to day complications in the classroom? As a teacher with 30 years of experience I can give seven reasons why merit pay won't work.

1. Standardized tests, such as the Ohio Graduation Test, test sophomores in the core subjects only. Is all the pressure on sophomore teachers of math, science, social studies, reading and writing? How will art, foreign language, and freshmen teachers be evaluated? Furthermore, sophomore core subject teachers have their students for less than seven months before testing. Are they responsible for everything their students have or have not learned from K-9?

2. Merit pay could be based on the number of students passing Advanced Placement tests, except my school doesn't offer AP courses, and it still leaves the physical education teacher out.

3. What is success? One teacher may work just as hard and creatively to get a struggling student to turn in his own six sentence paragraph as an AP English teacher does in getting his students to score fives on their AP exams.

4. Merit pay may lead to competition rather than cooperation among teachers. Would someone be as willing to share a great unit with a coworker? It could change the whole atmosphere of goodwill present in most schools.

5. What about cheating? Despite careful security, teachers are alone with students and test booklets at times during standardized testing week. What if those scores meant sending one's own child to college or even keeping one's job?

6. Teachers cannot control their classroom population. Some children are in and out of three different school districts within a single year. Just when a teacher feels he's making progress, the child is gone. And what about absences? The greatest lesson plan in the world won't help a student who chronically misses class. For a fair assessment of a teacher's effectiveness, he should be given the same students for at least two years. That rarely happens in most school systems.

7. Merit pay could be based on teacher evaluations. Principals usually sit in on classes and fill in forms. That's to assume no favoritism is involved and that all principals were once excellent teachers themselves.

Who is going to come up with a formula to include these and other variables? I'm sure other teachers could add to this list. Teaching is a messy profession and merit pay would make it even messier. In education, the focus should be on the students. If teacher incompetence is the concern, more rigorous certification and mentoring programs could be a solution.

DAY 33
Tattle Tail

"Mrs. Ball, Jessica's listening to her iPod," Mandy reported.

"Really? When I was in school it wasn't cool to tell on your classmates."

DAY 34
Off Topic

I love teaching the Bill of Rights to my government classes. Each amendment can be applied to current events and can evoke a good debate. I brought in a newspaper clipping about a high school girl who got suspended for violating the dress code by wearing a nose ring. She contested the suspension claiming the piercing was part of her religious practice and cited the First Amendment.

"So whose rights take priority," I asked the class, "the girl's or the school district's? Can she prove her religion is legitimate? If the school starts making exceptions can it maintain a dress code?"

Kelsey had an animated expression on her face and raised her hand. I was delighted to call on her pleased I had started a good classroom discussion. "Kelsey?"

"Did you cut your hair?" she asked.

I did a lousy job controlling my body language. "Thanks for noticing," I said, "but I was hoping for something about dress code or freedom of religion."

DAY 35
The Good Ones

I'd better put in a good word for the good students or someone will think I'm a pessimist. Sarah answers all the critical thinking questions, the ones after the multiple-choice and matching, the ones that most kids leave blank. Carol wants to be the first woman president and writes killer political speeches for practice. Harry and Ernest acted out the roles of Louis XIV and Jean-Baptiste Colbert and made history come alive in the classroom. Rick cleaned out his locker and handed me a bunch of No. 2 pencils. "Can you use these?" he asked.

"Thanks, Rick," I said. "No one ever gives me anything around here."

"You're my favorite teacher," he said.

"But Rick, you're in none of my classes."

DAY 36
Kindee-garten

"Ms. Ball, Wesley took my pencil," interrupted Myles.

"No I didn't, it's mine," whined Wesley.

I looked from one boy to the other. "I don't know how to handle problems like this. I'm not certified to teach kindergarten. You'll have to go downstairs to Miss Childers's room. Now we were on number 14. Justin, continue…"

DAY 37
Multi-Tasking

I gave a quiz that took 30 minutes of class time. I collected the papers, put them in a paperclip and set them on my desk. For the rest of the period I stood at the overhead projector and gave some introductory notes on the next topic. When the bell rang, Heather came up to me and asked, "Do you have our tests graded? Can I see what I got?"

DAY 38
On the Street

Tianna came to class without a belt. Teachers are supposed to enforce the dress code at all times with no exceptions. I opened my mouth to yell at her and send her to the office, but something made me leave her be. When I looked at her skinny child's frame and disheveled hair I let her slide right past me into her seat. She didn't have her American history text, homework, or notebook either. *That's not like her*, I thought, but twenty-five other kids took my attention, and I forgot about Tianna until the end of class.

"Mrs. Ball," she said, "I'm sorry I didn't have my work. Something happened yesterday and I couldn't get my books."

"What's up, Tianna?" There was a serious look on her face instead of the usual innocent glee. I told myself to stop and listen instead of attempting to get my own work done.

"My grandma and I had a fight last night and I ran away. She got mad at me for opening my report card before she got home. The police picked me up and I spent the night at the Lighthouse. I took the bus to school this morning and that's why I didn't have none of my stuff. I just didn't want you to think I was being disrespectful."

"Thanks for telling me. Where are you going after school today?"

"I have to take the bus back to the Lighthouse."

"Do you know where to catch it and do you have money?"

"I think so."

"Go to the office and tell Mrs. Stein. She'll make sure you know where to catch the bus."

It was Election Day. That afternoon I stood in front of the police station, a polling location, passing out fliers in support of our school levy. I saw Tianna walking the streets carrying a little plastic grocery bag with some clothes in it. It was cold and breezy and her coat was flying open. I told my colleague Cathy about her situation. We called to her.

"Tianna," I said. "Do you know where to catch your bus?"

"I'm not sure," she said.

"Go into the police station and find out," said Cathy.

She came out and reported to us. "I only have one token and I need two," she said.

Cathy pulled a five dollar bill out of her pocket and handed it to her. "Do you have any change?" said Tianna. "You have to have to have the exact amount or they won't let you on."

I had no idea how city buses worked. I hadn't ridden one in over fifty years. I didn't have a cent on me and my car was blocks away. Tianna ran into a Marathon gas station to get change then up the street to the bus stop.

"What is a fourteen-year-old child doing out on the street with no home and no one who cares about her?" said Cathy.

"That's a mystery," I said. "Tianna is as sweet as her name. I love her in class. She always participates and she doesn't even mind working with Donovan who stinks all the time."

"I know," said Cathy, "she's a doll baby for me too."

How could opening a report card be reason enough for her grandma to kick her out of the house? Besides, where is her mother? What the hell kind of cards has she been dealt?

When our shift was over, we handed the fliers to our replacements and parted ways. I wondered if Tianna made it to the Lighthouse and if I should have done something more for her. At 14 I went to a private school and had dinner every night with both parents. I headed to my new Honda. A filet mignon and Graeter's ice cream were waiting for me at home.

DAY 39
Name Calling

"Ms. Balls, Rodney called me a freak," shouted Jonathan as I was passing through the hallway."

"Well, are you one?" I asked.

"No."

"Then what are you worried about?"

DAY 40
Civil Disobedience

"Ms. Ball, Jake and them are making fun of my clothes," complained Robert.

"I know that's not right, but if you show them how much it upsets you, they'll keep doing it. The next time, say something like this, *Sorry you don't like them, they're very comfortable.* Then walk away. They'll be so surprised you didn't get mad they won't know what to do. It will be hard, but try it. Don't give other people power over you."

DAY 41
School Government

Democracy is the form of government in the United States. It means the majority rules. However, it does not exist in its classrooms. What exists is a dictatorship, the rule of one or a small group.

In many classrooms a few thugs have all the rights. Neither the teacher nor the well-behaved students have power. The thugs drain the teacher's energy and steal countless precious hours of academic learning time from the others.

Due process is followed when the thugs disrupt: parental contact is made, detentions and suspensions are assigned, and conferences are held to offer positive corrective strategies. They return to the classroom and disrupt. They are sent to the principal's office, the guidance counselor, and even to juvenile jail. They return and disrupt.

The reason education is poor is that it is often lowered to the level of a few dictators. Schools don't need more money or new teaching methods. They need an atmosphere conducive to learning. Nobody making policies seems to get it. A few kids are horrible.

Higher level activities would be implemented and quality would improve if the air were clear and teachers were allowed to teach. Often teachers give routine assignments to keep order and survive.

Democracy was established in the United States well-over two centuries ago. When will it reach the schools?

DAY 42
Time on My Side

I'd had it with Trevor. All during class I thought I'd done a remarkable job of not cussing at him, not laying a hand on him, and ignoring his total disruption of my lesson. Once again he broke my train of thought. I was desperate until I looked at the clock. There were only five minutes left in the bell before the kids switched classes. A revelation came to me; enlightenment, jubilation, ecstasy flowed through me. I looked right at him and said, "I only have to live with you for five more minutes. You have to live with yourself for the rest of your life."

DAY 43
Jolly Ranchers

It was 1:10 p.m. and sixth bell had been going on for only ten minutes. I had the low group of sophomores for Ohio Graduation Test social studies prep. What was I going to do with them for another forty-five minutes? The kids were not into the Spanish-American War. "This is lame," announced Austin.

"Thanks for the feedback," I said, "but this is going to be on the test in March and you must pass it to get your high school diploma. Everyone, read page 32 in your workbook and answer 3c, d, and e. Amy, get busy, we're going over this in ten minutes."

"I can't see right now. My eyes are dry," she replied.

"Does anyone have any lotion?" asked Daniel. "My hands are dry."

"I don't have a writing utensil," whined Caitlin. "David just ate mine."

"Ew," shouted Jake. "Wesley just ate a booger."

"Yeah," boasted Wesley, "a big juicy green one."

Oh my God, I thought. *Forty minutes left and the class has come apart. I've got to do something*. "Let's play a game!" I got out a bag of Jolly Ranchers and set it on my desk. The class became quiet and focused. I divided it into teams and started asking questions. "Team 1, what is the main idea behind the Spanish-American War?"

"Imperialism!" said Austin.

"Perfect. Point for Team 1. Team 2, what's imperialism?"

"It's when larger countries want to control smaller countries," stated Wesley.

"Great, point for Team 2. Team 3, why would a larger country want to control a smaller country?"

"Access to natural resources," said Amy.

"New markets for trade," added Caitlin.

"Military bases," chimed David.

"Outstanding! Point for Team 3. Team 4, what smaller country did not want to be controlled by what larger country?"

"Cuba was fighting for independence from Spain," Daniel said proudly.

"You got it." I pointed to the board. "All tied after round 1." I looked at the class and braced myself for a wisecrack, but everyone's eyes were on the bag of Jolly Ranchers. "Round 2," I continued.

It seemed the rest of the class went by in a minute. No one wanted to stop when I added the points. Students on the winning team got three Jolly Ranchers each. Second place students got two each, and everyone else got one for participating. I had them come up to my desk to pick their own flavors: blue raspberry, watermelon, grape, apple, or cherry.

Ron still sat in the back of the room. "Ron, don't you want one?" I asked.

"Sure, just toss me one."

"What color?"

"It doesn't matter."

I tossed him a grape. He leaned his head back and caught it in his mouth. The class cheered.

"Thank you, Mrs. Ball," they said, happily leaving the room. I looked at them in disbelief. How could their behavior and the quality of their statements have changed so drastically? I have power point presentations, videos, computer activities, and slide shows up my sleeve, but nothing ever worked like that $2.29 bag of Jolly Ranchers. Since Day 43 they have been a staple on my grocery list.

DAY 44
The Graduate

At 8 a.m. on Tuesday David sat at his desk with six or seven different pens laid out. Tyler noticed him carefully arranging them, picking them up for inspection, putting them down, taking them apart, putting them back together, and arranging them again. "All them pens," said Tyler, "and you never do no work."

Tyler was no one to talk, but he does a little more than David. In fact, no one in the whole school does less. The most David does with pens is just what Tyler observed. If he does manage to put ink on paper his writing is so illegible and incoherent I give him a C or D for the effort and pass him along. David is a senior now and will graduate in June. I don't know what his diploma will be worth, and can think of no employable skills he's attained. He has been passed along all these years because at some point, probably by the third grade, he's learned all he's capable of—reading, a little sloppy printing, and simple math. Good years have been wasted forced into a seat with books and paper and concepts he can't grasp. Not everyone needs to analyze a literary character's motives or whether U. S. actions in the Spanish American War were justified.

Why wasn't David removed from this torture and given suitable activities? He could wash cafeteria tables, run errands, change oil and tires, cut grass and shovel snow. Why do educators try and force square pegs into round holes year after year kid after kid? The school has taught him everything his brain could manage by grade four and then has tried to make a scholar out of him, thereby wasting the next seven years of his life. Teachers have worked with him and frustrated themselves and him, and have taken time and energy from students who will fit into round holes.

I'm one of those teachers. I met David when he was in the seventh grade. Determined to save him, I worked with him during my plan time for a whole year. "David," I said, "you've got to make spaces between your words. They all run together and I can't read what you write." Result? He still demonstrates the same resistance to any written work and the same few illegible incoherent sentences in answers to an assignment. Then I slap the same C or D on his paper to pass him on, give him a diploma, and get him out of here.

David sits in my senior government class playing with pens. That's what American education with its inclusion and mainstreaming has done for him.

Dylan, another senior almost as reluctant as David to do work, turned in this proposal for a 28th Amendment to the Constitution.

I think the 28th Amendment should be about a choice weather to join school or not. I think it should be a choice not something you have to do. Because school just ain't for someone like me. For example school just ain't for me.

DAY 45
Current Events

Tim is one of those kids who gets under my skin. He has a surly grin and a buzz hair cut. He sits in the back of the room and badgers me under his breath while I'm teaching. "Why?" "That's stupid." "How does she know?" "She's lame." Yes, I put him in the back, as far away from me as possible. I can picture his tall skinny body in a wife beater undershirt. For only eighteen years old, he's far too mean.

This morning the students were working on their current events questions. I cut articles out of the newspaper all week and tape them on the walls and white boards. Every Friday I hand out twelve questions and put the timer on for fifteen minutes. The students circulate around the room stopping at each article for answers.

"Tim, get busy," I said in a neutral voice. He was standing in the middle of the room talking loudly, his usual off topic agenda.

"I'm doing my work," he snarled.

"There are no news articles where you're standing," I said.

"Calm down," he told me.

"Tim, come out in the hall." *Stay in the critical thinking part of your brain*, I warned myself. *Don't jump into emotion.* "Your job is to do that assignment," I said, "and not to give me orders."

"Chill out, man."

"Don't give me orders."

"I was doing my work. I wasn't talking. You're just always…"

"The discussion is over. Go to the office."

I turned from him, went back into the classroom and slammed the door. I was shaking, and my heart and breathing were wild. Luckily, the others didn't notice and were still reading the articles. I got out an office referral and filled it in. There were still a few minutes left on the timer so I headed to the principal with the referral. Tim was still standing in the hall.

"Look, Mrs. Ball." I was not receptive to the story line he was beginning.

I squared my shoulders and looked right into his face. *This kid is not going to intimidate me today*, I told myself. "You are not in control in my classroom. And don't ever give me orders," I said.

He looked at the referral in my hand. I made a move toward the office.

"I'm sorry," he said.

I looked up at him in disbelief expecting more of his back talk. The skin on his face softened and I detected a trace of a human being underneath.

"I'll do my work and I won't say nothin' else."

I felt a trace of a human being inside me too. I turned and walked back to my room. He followed. I looked over my shoulder and held up the referral. "I'm putting this back in the drawer. I don't want to get it out again."

DAY 46
What's Important

What's important in a school system? The school board, the highest authority, certainly isn't. Most of its members have never been in a classroom and few have college degrees; yet they determine all the school's policies. School board members are parents who enable their lazy sons. The newest policy is that the basketball coach cannot bench their kids on the team who skip practice. The second in the chain of command is the superintendent. She means nothing to me. I rarely see her, and the emails she sends teachers about websites for supplemental materials and the latest directives from the Ohio Department of Education are a nuisance. Supplemental? I can't even put a dent in the textbook. The assistant superintendent is a giant pain in the ass. She creates busy work for teachers such as curriculum mapping, aligning lessons to the state standards, and data analysis. The homework she gives us takes hours, leaving little time to prepare our own lessons that could have an impact on our students. Both women rustle around the board office in their business suits, high heels and panty hose, playing corporate executive. The principal sits behind his desk in his secluded office and reads the sports section of the newspaper. The school day could go on perfectly fine without him.

So who are the vital players in a school building on any given day? Who else but the custodians would replace the fluorescent lights and wheel their carts around the building to clean up vomit and sticky juice? The secretary moves everyone around the building from 8 a.m. to 3 p.m. She runs the intercom, the bells, and the phones, and arranges for substitutes. It's horrible when the nurse is not in. She's the only one licensed to give the kids their medication. The whole place would explode if the kids didn't get their Ritalin. And where else would we send kids whining at our desks, the girls needing feminine products and the boys wanting ice for their jammed fingers from gym class? The assistant principal is the most overworked adult in the school. He runs back and forth from the middle school to the high school dealing with all the thugs who get kicked out of class.

What's important in the classroom? The textbooks aren't. Kids rarely bring them to the room after being issued a certain number on the first day of school. The books sit in lockers, rooms other than the one in which they are needed, and in the lost and found. Actually, teachers aren't even necessary. It doesn't take a college degree or a teaching certificate to do what I do all day. Any warm body, substitute or aide, could pick up paper, dirty Kleenex and broken pencils off of the floor. Any babysitter could answer the same incessant questions:

Can I have a Band-aid?

Do you have a safety pin?

Can I get a drink?

Can I go to the restroom?

What are we having for lunch?

When does this class end?

Where's the Kleenex?

Can I go to the nurse?

The Board of Education, the State Department of Education, the superintendent, and the assistant superintendent don't need to tell me what's important to kids. They could visit the classroom once in a while and see for themselves.

DAY 47
Survival

Driving home this afternoon I was churning the day over in my mind. I am not a nurse or a babysitter. I'm trained to teach academics. I have two master's degrees and it seems all I do is address basic needs. I would faint if anyone were to ask me, "What did you say the difference was between a presidential and parliamentary democracy?" or "Why did Martin Luther break away from the Catholic Church?"

Four miles from school I saw two of my students waiting for a bus. It was pouring down rain. They were jumping back and forth from the sidewalk to the curb. *What are those goofballs doing?* I stopped at the light and got a good look. They were running out to the curb to see if their bus was coming, then they quickly jumped away. The cars were speeding by splashing up water that was coming too fast for the gutters to drain. Over and over they ran out to the street then back to the sidewalk. I sat at the light in my brand new silver Honda with heated leather seats and satellite radio watching Myaa and Nolan. I realized what they were doing. They were trying not to miss their bus, and they were trying not to get drenched.

This was a living example of that Bloom's Taxonomy pyramid hanging in my classroom. The pyramid starts at the lowest level of intellectual behavior, the recognition of facts. It progresses through more complex levels such as analysis and synthesis to the highest level, evaluation. Unless basic needs are met, higher order thinking cannot take place. When kids are hungry, sick, or tired they cannot rise beyond the lowest levels. *Survival,* I thought, *that's what's important to kids.* They're no different from teachers who value the custodian more than the superintendent. Some students live ten miles from school and have to transfer buses twice. I never realized the amount of energy it took for some students just to get to and from school. They don't have their own cars, and their parents aren't available to pick them up and drive them home.

The next day I deleted emails from the board office and thanked the custodian, secretary, and nurse for their invaluable services. In the classroom I gave out Band-aids and Kleenex a little more graciously, still trying to get to the next level on Bloom's pyramid.

DAY 48
Tasty Text

"Ms. Ball, how much do them government books cost?" asked Brandy the first thing on Monday morning.

"Fifty dollars, why?"

"My dog ate this one." She held it out to me. It didn't resemble the brand new *Government Alive* text I issued her at the beginning of the year. The front cover was torn off and there were teeth marks and brown stains all over it. I didn't want to touch it. I hate dogs, especially ones that destroy my precious textbooks.

"Brandy, I've been teaching for twenty-five years and I never believed the *dog ate my work* excuse until now." She grinned. I examined the book still holding my distance. "Don't you ever feed your dog? It looks like he was really hungry for the glue at the binding."

"Yes, Ms. Ball, I feed him."

"What kind of a dog is this?"

"He's a Doberman."

"What's his name?"

"King."

"Is he big?" She stretched out her arm to show he came to my waist. "Wow, I'd be petrified of King. I'm never coming to your house. He seems vicious."

"He ain't. Want to see a picture of him?"

"Sure," I said. I couldn't have cared less about her dog and I was busy getting ready for class. But I'd never seen Brandy so enthusiastic and I didn't want to discourage her.

In the picture I could see Brandy and King posing on the sofa in her living room, her brown arms around his black neck. Her big smile and the whites of King's eyes lit up the photo.

"You're both beautiful," I said. "But now I know I'm never ringing your doorbell." Brandy was pleased.

Since I found something to kid her about every morning, Brandy lays her head on her desk less often and uses her mangled book more. Maybe since I showed a little interest in something she loved, she is showing a little more interest in government.

I won't put the book on the fine list. Brandy doesn't have the money to pay for it, and the office will never hold her to it.

Notice to all teachers! The *dog ate my work* story is possible; and if you want better student performance, ask questions about the dog that ate it.

DAY 49
Roaches: Bugs, Clips and Me

My student teacher from Miami University had just completed his experience in my classroom. Although he was a big help, I was relieved to have my room back to myself. I could teach as lousy as hell again and no conscious adult would know about it. I wrote Tim a nice evaluation and threw him a party in the teachers' lounge. The next day my principal approached me, "Xavier University called. Can you take a student observer for the month of November?"

"Sure," I said, knowing that colleges are always in need of placements for future teachers. Although the college kids are energetic and have new ideas and skills, it's still a pain to host them. I hate being on display. I'm supposed to be a highly qualified teacher (HQT), that is, model good teaching strategies, dress like a professional, and control behavior. *Here I go again. Someone besides me will know how bad I am.*

Andrew from Xavier University came to me the first morning of the second quarter. I was starting the unit on the Indian Independence Movement and planned background information before showing the movie *Gandhi*. I thought I had a good lesson and would look fairly competent in front of Andrew. I prepared a pyramid showing the caste system of India, a two-column chart comparing the Hindu and Muslim religions, a map of India labeled with the major cities, and pictures of the Taj Mahal.

Andrew observed me from the back of the room. He was tall and studious-looking in his khaki slacks, light blue oxford shirt, and navy blazer. I hoped I looked good to him and that he was impressed with the information I was giving the kids.

I hadn't even finished the first transparency when I heard a ruckus from the row by the white board. "A roach just crawled out of Charles' pocket," announced David. Charles was on his knees looking under the chair and on the floor. He was trying to let the class know that the roach came from anywhere but his pocket.

"It wasn't me," he kept saying. He was determined to find it and would not sit down. The kids were laughing and screaming. There I stood by my overhead projector and transparencies. The Indian Independence Movement didn't stand a chance against Charles and the roach. I must have looked like a goon to Andrew. He was probably thinking, *She's an experienced teacher? This class is out of control.*

Then Donald yelled across the room, "Maybe you can get it with a roach clip."

"Go to the office." I'd had enough of Donald so far this year with his frequent references to drugs. On Halloween he came dressed as a drug dealer and went around asking kids if they wanted some crack. He had just been readmitted to school after a six-month expulsion for raping a girl in the back of the auditorium.

"Hey, what'd I do?" he said giving high-fives to kids as he left the room.

"Bye, Donald," they sang. Charles sat down relieved that someone had stolen the spotlight.

"Let's get back to our notes," I urged. "The Hindus believe in many gods, whereas the Muslims…"

"I can't take notes," blurted Bernice, "I don't have a pencil." She opened up her large purse and rummaged through it. Out spilled an iPod, make-up, lotion, a brush, a cell phone, and fried chicken wrapped in tinfoil.

The kids were fascinated. "Hey," shouted Casey, "you can feed the chicken to the roach!"

Everyone howled. My confidence and train of thought were broken. I stuttered and stumbled through the rest of the transparencies, not daring to look at Andrew. I wanted to be that roach and crawl silently out of the room.

DAY 50
Juicy Jargon

Tyrell sat at his desk so still and read the note so intensely I knew it was a juicy one. No way could he be reading about the Russian Revolution. As I reached to snatch it from him he quickly tossed it on Khardiatou's desk. "It ain't mine," he said. "Khardi asked me to read it for her."

She covered it with her hand but I pulled it away. "You're both off task," I said. "I don't care whose it is."

The frayed piece of notebook paper was folded in eighths. I opened it and noticed a yellow stain at the bottom. My eyes must have gotten big as I began reading, for Khardi pleaded in her broken English. "It's not mine. I found it in the bathroom. You know I can't write."

Khardi is an ESL student from Senegal. She doesn't have the skills to string sentences together, and for once it worked in her favor.

Dear Baby,

This is your baby. I miss you and love you. I love when I suck your dick and when you push my head down and put it in my mouth it taste so good. I love it. Baby I am shy but, that shouldn't stop you from doing what you do to me. Don't let my shyness stop you. I want you to touch me like you do I love you, you are my life I don't love nobody but you. Every day I wake up I think about you when I go to sleep I think about you and dream about you. When I go to school I think about you. Baby I can't stop thinking about you. The first time I see you it was love at first sight. I don't care if you ugly or not I don't look at the face I look at your heart. When we get married its going to be a good life. I just can't wait until you say will you marry me.

I folded the note gingerly and stuck it in my desk drawer trying not to imagine what the yellow stain might be. "No, Khardi, I know you didn't write this, and Tyrell doesn't need to read it to you. Get back to your worksheet."

At the end of the day I got out the note and examined it more carefully. I narrowed it down to a freshman girl, Ashley, who slants her s's like those on the paper. I knew right away who her baby was. She hangs around his locker, and I see them arm and arm in the hall with that glazed look. I want to tell her she's in for a miserable life if she gets her wish. I've known Jamel, the tall senior, a lot longer than she has. He's made my life miserable in the classroom for the past five years. I remembered the day he punched Tyler during U.S. studies. I lost a whole hour of instruction while the principal and resource officer questioned me and the rest of the class. The only reason he hasn't been expelled is that he's on an IEP, a special designation given to kids with learning and/or behavior problems. They have more leeway than regular students when it comes to discipline. It would take nothing less than murder to get rid of an IEP kid.

I caught myself before tossing the note into the garbage can. I found a small manila envelope and put it back in the drawer. The next time I need to keep Ashley in line I'll get it out and ask her if she wants me to show it to her mother.

DAY 51
Parent Involvement

Sheldon has had it with me. "Man, you get on my nerves. I'm going to get my mama in here on you," he said.

"Good," I replied, "I've been trying to get in touch with her for two weeks."

DAY 52
No Exit

Amanda came to my desk jiggling and hopping from one foot to the other. "I have to go to the bathroom, it's an emergency."

"Okay, give me your hall pass to sign."

"I forgot it in my locker."

"You can go, but you owe me a ten minute detention after school for not having it with you."

"Never mind," she said. Amanda immediately stopped jiggling and walked back to her seat."

DAY 53
Double Meaning

To enrich my unit on the Civil War, I thought I'd read *Red Badge of Courage* with the 7th graders. Stephen Crane had quite a command of the English language. He used dense phrases such as *outer portals of the mind,* and words I could hardly pronounce or define such as *accouterments, imprecations, and perfunctorily.* Many of the sentences were impossible, for example, *He dreaded to place some unscrupulous confidant upon the high plane of the unconfessed from which elevation he could be derided.* The book was certainly too dry and difficult for my students. After the first two chapters I realized I had made the wrong choice. The kids were not into the story, and I knew I was inviting discipline problems. I should have simply collected the books and begun something else, but me—once I start something, I'm determined to finish it.

Usually the students take turns reading, but because *Red Badge of Courage* was so sophisticated, I ended up reading most of it to the class myself. One afternoon we were all practically asleep when I heard myself in Crane's words, *"I'll carry the flag into battle!" ejaculated the youth.* I flinched then peered over my paperback to see if anyone got it. The word went past everyone except for two big boys, Patrick and James. They looked at each other then smothered their laughter in their hands. I hid my face behind my book and fought as hard as they not to break up.

When the bell rang I said, "Patrick and James, could you stay back for a minute?" They stood in front of my desk still grinning while I waited for the room to clear. "I appreciate the way you both handled yourself when I read that word. *Ejaculate* also means exclaim. Look it up while I write you a late pass." They eagerly paged through the dictionary.

"We see, Ms. Ball," they said pointing to the word.

"I wish you'd look up all your vocabulary that enthusiastically," I said handing them the note. Snickering and nudging each other, they left the room.

DAY 54
Out of Shape

This morning I walked my sixth graders from the library on the first floor back up to our classroom on the third floor. On the second floor Josh got out of line and leaned against the railing, doubled over and out of breath.

"What's the matter, Josh? I'm 40 years older than you and I can make it up the steps."

"Man," he said, "I gotta quit smokin'."

DAY 55
Alliteration

I had my reading group in a circle and we were enjoying the children's classic, *Tuck Everlasting*. My tongue slipped and I referred to Miles, Jesse, Mae, and Angus Tuck as the Fuck Family. There was a brief silence as the sixth graders processed what they just heard. Stifled snickers accelerated into uncontrolled laughter. There was nowhere to hide or nothing to do but laugh along. "Please don't go home and tell your parents I said the F word," I said.

DAY 56
Last Resort

The class was particularly rowdy this afternoon. I couldn't settle the kids down for anything. I changed their seats, sent two boys to the office, and passed out an easy fun worksheet. "If you're not quiet," I yelled, "I'll get fired for not being able to control my class. Tomorrow you'll have someone in here meaner than me." The kids focused on their paper and I got through the rest of the day.

DAY 57
Trench Warfare

Fourth bell is the bell from hell. It is composed of twenty high school juniors and seniors, fifteen of whom are boys. Male ego and testosterone pulsate throughout the room vying for the attention of the five girls. There is no way to make a seating chart. There are only four corners to the room and twice the amount of loudmouths. The four worst are Charles, Kenny, Tommy, and Terry. They wear grills, play sports, and have an inflated sense of their self-worth. Most of the other students are followers. They provide an audience for the big four, laugh at their acts, and don't have enough sense to think for themselves. The boys are especially disruptive on Mondays and Fridays, Mondays rehashing the results of Friday's game, and Fridays making predictions for the upcoming game.

One Friday before the football game there was more hype than usual. Madison was playing Washington, the local rival. "Man, we gonna woop their ass tonight," shouted Kenny across the room to Charles.

"Yeah, with you, me, Antwan, and Josh we'll win for sure," Charles yelled back.

"We're going to State this year," Terry bragged.

"I'd like to start class," I said. "Yesterday we were talking about World War I soldiers and their life in the trenches."

Charles turned to Tacha. "So what are you doing this weekend?"

"Class is going on," I asserted.

"There ain't no class going on," said Charles.

"Go to the office."

"This is stupid. I'm going to hit her. This is why kids don't come to school."

Charles slammed his binder on the desk and gave Eric a high-five. He left the room amid the laughter and applause of the class.

I tried to move on. "Who can give an example of what it was like in the trenches? You have about eight conditions in your notes from yesterday."

"I wish Mr. Downy was here," whined Terry. "He was so fun."

Mr. Downy was my cool young student teacher from first quarter. "Mr. Downy got a job in Minnesota and is not coming back, so let's continue. Remember how the trenches were dug? What caused the soldiers' confusion? Demetrius."

"What you call on me for? I don't know nothin' about that."

Tommy called over to Kenny. "Did you check out Mr. Graham's student teacher? She's fine."

"You mean the babe with the long blond hair? I'm going to get it on with her," said Kenny.

"Go the office." *What makes you think she'd want to get it on with you?*

Kenny pimp-walked out of the room. The class cheered. I was shook up. I hate sending kids to the office. Good teachers handle their own discipline problems through their innate charisma and masterful lessons. "The trenches were not dug in straight lines. They were like a maze. When the soldiers lost their direction they didn't know if they were in a friendly trench or an enemy trench. Robert, be quiet."

"What you say something to me for? I'm not the only one talking." I was lost. I couldn't send a third student out. What would the administration think of me? I had to keep moving.

"Boredom was another problem. How did the soldiers fill in the hours between battles?" I looked out at all the bored faces. There was no response from anyone. "They read books, smoked, wrote letters, and played cards. Another condition was flooded trenches." I was drowning. I had to think of a way out before the next enemy attack. "The stagnant water brought diseases and trench foot. What vermin infested the trenches and relentlessly aggravated the soldiers?" I looked out and waited. No enemy fire, but no response either. "Does anyone remember about the rats and lice?" I was lost and drowning and trapped in a pit with vermin. The enemy was getting ready to fire. I couldn't fire back with another referral or I would be fired. "The rats ate the soldiers' bread which caused starvation, another condition we talked about yesterday." It occurred to me. The kids were starved, too—for attention and stimulating activities. They're going into the trenches, and I'm coming out.

I walked into the middle of the room. "This is no-man's land. What's no-man's land?" Some paged through their notebooks for the definition.

"It's the strip of territory along the Western Front that separated opposing armies."

"Outstanding! Thanks, Terry."

I counted off 1,2,1,2. "Ones, you're the Germans. Go to the window side of the room. Twos, you're the French. Go to the white board side. Arrange the desks into trench lines and crouch under them for protection." I was heartened. The kids did what I said. "I will ask a question and the side that answers correctly may advance one foot. If the side misses, it must retreat. The army that has gained the most ground in no-man's land after all my questions is the winner. You can fire paper wads at the enemy, but remember, the only way to gain ground is to get the question right."

"I'm the general. Get your trench in order," commanded Eric.

"We're the Germans," said Kim. "Let's win this war and mess up history."

Robert fired a paper wad at the French. "Gas. Gas. Get your masks on," yelled Mark.

The bell rang. "Can we play this tomorrow?" asked several students.

"Yes. I will make up questions from your notes. Study them for homework so you will be prepared to advance. And I will bring cookies to ease your starvation after the battle."

DAY 58
Letters from the Lost Generation

Since when do letters on dirty wrinkled paper with cuss words and abrupt endings receive the highest grades? It's perfectly fine as long as they're dated any time between June, 1917 and November, 1918, and the return address is Allied Headquarters, Compiègne, France.

Students in U.S. studies, pretending to be WWI soldiers, came up with some great ideas to authenticate their letters home from the trenches. They communicated to their families about the conditions under which they had to fight. They fired machine guns from muddy trenches, smelling of sweat and rotting bodies and infested with lice, frogs, and rats. Constant enemy shelling and fear of gas attacks caused daily stress and trauma.

Tammy Johnson dipped her letter in coffee and baked it in the oven to simulate an artifact from a muddy trench. Ryan Creed wrote a letter of condolence to the mother of a comrade while crushing a rat with his heavy boot. Some soldiers read the Bible to boost their morale.

Students captured the spirit of the "Lost Generation," soldiers so affected by the horrors of warfare they were unable to adjust to civilian life after the Armistice. Almost everyone was successful with the test questions on WWI. They are now learning how the Treaty of Versailles and the League of Nations did not settle prewar conflicts and only lead to the rise of Hitler and WWII. Students are left with open ended questions: *How could six wars follow the "War to End All Wars"* and *Could WWII have been avoided had the U.S. joined the League of Nations?*

DAY 59
Past and Present

To finish my unit on WWI I take the kids through a lengthy explanation of the Balfour Declaration. It was issued by the British government in 1917 to support a national homeland for the Jews in Palestine. Mandy huffed, "More boring facts. This has no meaning in my life. Why do we have to take history? I am never going to use the Balfour Declaration for anything." She glared at me, challenging me to justify wasting her time with such tedium.

"Was 9/11 important in your life?" I asked.

"Yes."

"Do you think Arab terrorists just woke up one day and decided to fly our airplanes into the Pentagon and World Trade Center?"

"I guess not."

"Do you think there might be some history involved in 9/11?" She rolled her eyes, laid her head on the desk and turned it towards the window. I turned to the rest of the class. "The Balfour Declaration is part of the history behind 9/11."

"How?" Ben saved me.

"It's complicated, but I'll try and give you a basic idea. Remember I said that the Balfour Declaration supported a homeland for the Jews in Palestine. But this territory was occupied 80% by Arabs. They felt their homes and lemon tree orchards were being invaded."

"So?" A couple of voices indicated some interest.

"So who attacked the U.S. on 9/11."

"Al-Qaida," said Ben. "And isn't that an Arab terrorist organization?"

"Correct."

"So why are the Arabs mad at the U.S.?" asked Tracy.

"Britain issued the Balfour Declaration but the U.S. supported it. Britain and the U.S. have been close allies through both World Wars, and Britain is one of the few countries backing up President Bush in Iraq right now."

"So Arab terrorists hate the U.S. because we support the Jews?" asked Ben.

"Exactly."

Mandy's head came up. "Why do the Arabs hate the Jews?" I couldn't have been more pleased with her question.

"The Arabs and the Jews have been fighting over control of Palestine since the first century A.D. They both view it as their national state. So 9/11, something most of you admit affected you personally, had to do with boring historical events."

"I guess they're not so boring anymore," she admitted.

As the lesson was going better than it started, an idea came to me. "For the next half hour, I want you to write a journal entry about your experience on 9/11. Where were you? What were you doing? How did you find out? What was the weather like? What were your feelings as you watched the scene over and over on TV? How did members of your family react? How did your country change?"

The kids didn't hesitate to delve into their writing to recall a vivid day in their personal lives. When the bell was over I collected their stories. "Tomorrow we'll have time to read some out loud in class. You have just come alive to history. You have chosen to become an informed citizen of this country and understand the meaning of current events. Now you'll be able to explain 9/11 to your children and grandchildren."

DAY 60
Pens and Pencils

The most frustrating part of teaching is the phenomena of, the lack of, the act of, a student coming into the classroom with something to write with. It is truly an unsolvable problem. Every Saturday morning at Kroger I buy several 10-packs of Bic pens and a 20-pack of #2 pencils. By Tuesday morning there isn't one in sight. There's no work in sight either. The standard excuse is, "I don't have nothin' to write with." These same kids come into the room well supplied with iPods, cell phones, combs and brushes, lotion, make-up, and gum. But a pen or pencil? Out of the question.

I've tried various strategies over the years to conquer this seemingly simple problem. Printed in bold letters on my syllabus is: *Be prepared. Bring a pen or pencil to class.* I emphasize this at the beginning of every school year and give the students my usual lecture. "It is not my responsibility to supply you each day. I don't ask you to do my work. Just be responsible for your own." The concept lasts just about as long as my tirade.

One teacher suggested exchanging a personal item for a borrowed pencil. Take a key ring or shoe as insurance you'll get your pencil back at the end of class. I found the students would rather skip their work and keep their belongings or, that when the bell rings, we both forget and the pencil leaves my class anyway and their crap clutters my desk. Later, I'm forced to give the belonging back without receiving mine of course. Besides, the exchange takes too much time and energy from the thought process of my lesson.

I've tried delayed gratification. Let the student suffer through the bell without a pen or pencil once, and he's sure to have it the next day. The kid either disrupts class because there's nothing else to do, or he lays his head on the desk and goes to sleep. I end up being the one in trouble since the principle doesn't allow kids sleeping or kicked out into the hallway.

I've tried just being gracious by keeping the cylinder cup on my desk full of pens and pencils. But it doesn't matter if I have 200 in there or just one, the cup is empty by mid morning.

Where do all those pens and pencils go? Pockets, lockers, garbage cans? I have given special Constitution pencils and shiny Star Student ones as rewards for reciting the Preamble or for perfect homework. I order them from a catalog with my own money. It breaks my heart when I recognize them on the floor in the hallway broken in half.

Today my silver Cross pen was missing. I carefully hid it under a notebook on my desk, and when I went back to write with it, it was gone. My sister gave it to me when I got my master's degree. She had my name engraved on it. I looked on the floor, in my desk, and finally retraced every step I took so far that day. I went to the copying machine in the office, the teachers' lounge, and the restroom. I returned to my room devastated that I lost my sister's cherished gift that I managed to keep for 20 years.

The students were taking a test. I walked among the desks to see if anyone had a question and spotted my silver Cross. "George, where did you get that pen?"

He looked up at me and then at the pen in his hand. "Oh, I borrowed it from your desk, Ms. Ball. I couldn't find nothin' else to write with. I'll give it back when I'm done."

"Here," I said. "Let's trade." I gave him a Kroger Bic. I clutched my precious pen in my hand, the symbol of my sister, my master's degree, and my 25 years in the classroom. George continued to write not knowing the difference.

DAY 61

Silenced by Insult

Shauna is talking to Colleen seated behind her. "Shauna, please keep quiet," I tell her politely.

"You ain't say nothn' to Tommy and Aaron, they talkin' too."

"You're right, but you're the loudest. Once you're quiet, I'll work on them. I can't get everyone at once."

"That's bull," snaps Shauna, turned around in her seat still talking to Colleen.

They start snickering about my name. "Mrs. Balls, ha, ha. Did you hear that? Mrs. Balls."

"I heard it girls. Right now I'm trying to teach high school history. You're not the first to think of putting an s on my last name. My fourth graders thought of it 25 years ago when I was downstairs teaching reading."

Shauna turns and faces the front of the room, and Colleen readies her materials for note taking.

DAY 62
Silenced by Shock

I stepped outside my room between bells today for a change of scenery when Bianca approached. "Mrs. Ball," she said, "Brittany told me to tell you she's in the bathroom, and she'll be a little late."

Jamal was standing there listening and swinging a heavy load of keys on a long chain. "Yeah, I bet Brittany in there playin' with her little thingie."

Shocked and embarrassed, I didn't know what to do or say. There was no use writing a referral on Jamal. He wasn't disrupting class, but just talking normally for a kid with no filter or sense of boundaries.

I could have made a case for sexual harassment. Instead, I played dumb, motioned Bianca and Jamal into the room, and started my lesson.

DAY 63
What's the Hurry?

My 6th graders were in line on the playground after lunch recess. I started to walk them into the building and back to the classroom. Robert was upset and holding up the line. "Mrs. Ball, he cutted!"

"Robert, stop and think. You're going to the room to do work. You're not in line to ride the Beast at Kings Island. Do you necessarily care who gets there first?"

DAY 64
Transfer Student

Amanda was sitting in the office with her third discipline referral in a week. "I'm going to a different school, this school sucks," she announced.

"Good for you," I said. "You know, I read in a book that wherever you go, you take yourself with you."

DAY 65
Good Ole Boys

Mr. Hoffman, "Hoff," never reads his students' papers. He slaps an A on every one and everyone gets an A in his history classes. The kids either love him for the easy A, or hate him for learning nothing. He's also the athletic director and spends class time talking to the athletes about game plans, results, and stats. The little work he does require of the students consists of worksheets from the text chapters. As long as they're turned in, filled in, with name at the top, it's an A. By the time the school year ends, the kids will have watched *Pearl Harbor* at least six times. Besides sports, Hoff likes to talk about good restaurants, the 60s, and his service in Vietnam.

Hoff is one of the Good Ole Boys, along with Mr. Howard the principal, Mr. Finan the phys. ed. teacher, and Mr. King the science teacher. They're all big white males, Baby Boomers, who run the school by reading the newspaper at their desks, slapping each other on the back, talking about sports, and play fighting with the top male athletes. The women and the younger men actually teach from 8 a.m. to 3 p.m. and are held accountable for it.

Amber, one of Mr. Hoffman's world history students, set out to prove he never reads his students' work. For one of his assignments, instead of discussing the causes and consequences of the French Revolution, Amber wrote how boring Hoff's classes are and how he never reads anything the students turn in. She pushed her theory to the limit by sprinkling her "essay" with cuss words including the F one.

Sure enough Hoff returned it to her with a big red A at the top. Amber promptly showed it to her classmates and took it home to her mother who promptly showed it to the superintendent. Amber's "essay" was the talk of the teachers' lounge for a few days. We teachers, not members of the Good Ole Boys Club, wondered what would happen to Hoff.

It turned out nothing. I was punished instead. Amber was simply transferred out of Hoffman's class and into mine. So I was stuck with the brat for the rest of the year, and Hoff was allowed to remain a Good Ole Boy.

I couldn't punish Hoff, but I made it a point to let Amber know that her little scheme backfired. I scrutinized each of her papers and returned them for a rewrite if they were anything less than perfect.

DAY 66
Good Old Hoff

As Amber sat in my class, pretty and innocuous looking enough, I kept my guard, ever suspicious of what else she could be scheming. It was evident, from the grammar and content of the "essay" she turned into Hoff and the ones I received, that she hadn't learned much in anyone's class. When she rolled her eyes at my suggestions to improve her work, I could see that she was no more interested in getting a good education than Hoff was in giving one.

Unlike Amber though, you can't help but like Hoff. Jovial, with a big heart, the Jolly Green Giant is always giving kids rides and money. There's nothing creepy about this; he just feels sorry for their socioeconomic circumstances. Despite his wealth of knowledge of history, he spends his afternoons calling coaches from other schools and scheduling games. He puts new instructional materials in my mailbox knowing I'll do a better job teaching them than he. I hesitate going to his room to thank him because I can never get away. He talks my free bell away about the many teams, sports, and winning seasons he's coached as well as his dinner date the night before. One time he tried to talk me into writing his curriculum map, and even offered me a generous payment to do so. I told him I'd pay someone to get me out of that odious administrative directive.

One year I took my government class downtown to City Hall for an all day student workshop. In the morning session Sylvia got sick in the middle of the county commissioner's speech. She was in no shape to tough the rest of the day out. Not wanting to leave and have the others miss the mock trial and tour of the justice center, I was in a jam. I called school and asked if Hoff could come and rescue me. As sure as the As on all the papers, Hoff pulled up in front of City Hall. He laid a blanket in the back of his van and escorted Sylvia home. Thanks to Hoff we were able to enjoy the afternoon session.

You can count on Hoff, too, when it comes to standardized test scores. When I get his kids from the previous year, it's a given I can't possibly teach my year's worth of history while making up for his. When the state scores come in around mid-May, it's very convenient to blame the poor results on Hoffman. The history department dreads the day he retires because we won't have Hoff "to kick around anymore." Sharp as any teacher of American history, he would take no offense to our reference to Richard Nixon. The Good Ole Boy is really a good old boy.

DAY 67
Test Results

Mr. Fischer, our superintendent, was in my class speaking to the kids about the importance of the Proficiency Tests. "Each one of you counts as three percentage points for the district," he said. "We need 75% of you to score a 75% or higher on all five tests. This will give Madison the necessary indicators and a high ranking on the school report card. It's important that you work hard and listen to your teachers these next few weeks."

I looked around the room. Destiny was turning her eyelids inside out and Heather was pulling strands of her long blond hair in front of her face and inspecting the ends with the tips of her fingers. CJ was mesmerized by a piece of fuzz that he repeatedly blew into the air, and Mark was taking apart his ball point pen and arranging the parts on his desk. How Madison scores on the Proficiency Tests is not a big part of their lives.

DAY 68
Empty Desk Full Mouth

A lot of kids come to class empty handed like honored guests: no book, no notebook, no homework, no pen or pencil. I call it the empty desk syndrome. Today out of a class of 22 students, four had their homework. It's frustrating going over questions and calling on the same four students while the rest are unengaged. Sean had an empty desk, but chose to engage himself nevertheless. When Daniel read the wrong answer from his notebook, Sean interjected loudly, "Man, that is so lame!"

I glared at Sean. "How is Daniel's effort worse than your zero? The only failures I see are those with empty desks. Sean, you need to work on having an empty mouth and a full desk."

DAY 69
Sounds of School

"Ms. Balls, get him, he's messin' with me."

"She's talkin' about my Mama."

"Man, I gotta use it."

"My stomach hurts."

"My homework is at home."

"Shut up."

"No, you shut up."

"It wasn't me."

"Steven's gay."

"Patrick hit me."

"My neck burns."

"This class sucks."

"That's a smack."

"You have issues."

"You're trippin'."

"Chill out."

"What's crack-a-lackin'?"

"All tatted up."

"Psyche, naw."

"Got that wad."

"What time do we get out of here?"

DAY 70
Foreign Exchange

Today I had to take Yu to school. Not y-o-u, but Y-u, Yu Takada from Japan. Cheryl, who's in charge of the foreign exchange program, called me late last night. She had a workshop and wouldn't be able to get Yu to Madison. Would I take him? I had just gotten home from my parents after putting my mother to bed. *Oh boy, I certainly don't need anyone else to take care of.*

Of course, I said yes and got up a half hour earlier to accommodate them. Yu was waiting in Cheryl's driveway. He peered into the window of my car before opening the door. *Oh my God, what am I going to say to a fifteen-year-old boy from Japan?* I had no concept of any Asian language and I knew that Yu struggled with English. It was raining and still pitch dark. I needed to focus on driving safely, but instead I was racking my brain for a way to communicate with him. I wanted Yu to feel comfortable and I didn't want to seem unfriendly. After his, "Thank you for taking me," and my "You're welcome," there was that awkward silence I dreaded.

Instead of watching the road, I looked over at him. "How many brothers and sisters do you have?" I said it in a loud voice, as if that would compensate for the language barrier. I was relieved to hear him answer. He said he had a brother named Yoshihiro and a sister named Toshiko. *Now what? Let's see, Japan, islands.* I asked him what island he was from and to name all of them.

"Hokkaido, Honshu, Shikoku, and Kyushu," he said. *Oh good, I'm getting through.* I thought it wise to stick to concrete proper nouns instead of abstract ideas such as, "Do you miss your family?" or "How do you like American schools?"

I was crippled. He, the child, had to meet me in my language, and I, the adult, couldn't even attempt to meet him in his. My master's degree in French was useless.

Yu had his electronic translator on his lap. With it he graciously kept up his end of the conversation. He asked me when my birthday was, and how many years I'd been teaching. The only thing I could offer him was an affirmation of his English, and a fluent model of mine. When he said, "I ha un bigger broder," I said, "Oh yes, you have one older brother." I had to keep reminding myself to watch the road. An accident would be far worse than any moment of silence.

When we pulled into the parking lot he thanked me again. On the way to the building he scrambled to pick up some folders I dropped and rushed to open the door for me. We parted down different hallways. Although I was exhausted from the trip, this Japanese boy with the shiny black hair heartened me. His manners, and his courage and ambition to spend a year overseas, were impressive. Foreign exchange students are quite exceptional, I thought, as I passed our kids slouching against their lockers. Instead of electronic translators, they were absorbed with their iPods and cell phones. I could just picture Zac over there in a school in Japan. How would, "Pull up your pants," or "Get your head off the desk," sound in Japanese?

When I got to my homeroom, I asked the kids how you compliment someone these days. I knew "beasty" and "gangsta" were out. Tabitha told me to say, "You're the truth."

"What?"

"It's fine, Mrs. Ball, just say it."

I wrote a little note and had her take it down to Yu's class. It said:

Yu, I enjoyed the ride. You're the truth.

DAY 71
Hall Duty

Picture a teacher walking through the halls each morning cheerfully greeting each student with a little banter thrown in:

"Hi, Justin, you're good and early today. Why don't you shock me and go get your homework ready for second bell."

"Now, Ms. Ball, I wouldn't want to give you a heart attack or anything."

"I'll worry about my health. You worry about your grade."

Forget that scenario. No use greeting anyone when I walk the halls each morning to serve my duty. Kids have iPods in their ears and eyes glued to cell phones cupped in their hands. I am invisible. No one hears me or sees me. They are too absorbed in their technology to acknowledge my presence.

With utmost self-importance they stare at their phones in the most serious manner as if they were the president addressing a national security crisis, or a doctor communicating a cutting edge treatment to another doctor to save someone's life. Or they're bopping to the music on their iPods, oblivious to their surroundings. The message is, *"Don't bother me. I'm busy with more important things than you."*

"Okay, I won't," I reply to myself. *"It makes hall duty easier. I don't have to tell anyone to quiet down or break up a fight. They're doing all the talking and fighting on their Blackberry or whatever."* I'm not into or impressed with their gadgets.

One day when I had the kids in the classroom and the cells and iPods had to be put away, I asked them what they're always so absorbed with on those little flashing screens. They told me about their codes, certainly not resembling wartime intelligence. Here is their intelligence:

LOL- laugh out loud

BRB- be right back

IDK- I don't know

WTF- what the fuck

OMG- oh my God

LMAO- laugh my ass off

ROFL- roll on the floor laughing

I agree. IDK. No, you don't know the fundamental social skill of greeting a teacher when you pass her in the hall.

I agree. LOL. Yes, I laugh out loud at the way you think you're so important just because you own a cell phone. You look like a five-year-old playing dress ups or army. You don't need that technology for anything. You have no degree, job, or position of authority. You need to do your homework and get your high school diploma first.

I agree. WTF. What the fuck are you doing? You look like you're having a seizure gyrating to music no one else can hear.

The 2008 presidential election is over and Obama won. Maybe that's trying to tell me something. The young fresh stallion has beaten the old warhorse McCain. Maybe I need to retire and let the young deal with the young. Obama's 2.0 is a vast web network to reach out to the public, especially the youth. Let the president talk to these kids in cyberspace. I'm going to visit my old parents in person and then I'm going home to read a book. I don't like music piped directly into my ears and I don't even know where my cell phone is. When I say TTYL, I mean *talk* to you later, not *text* to you later.

DAY 72
Rich Material

"Since local politics aren't as glamorous as national politics, we're going to switch it up this chapter," I told my students in senior government. "Get into your groups and we'll tackle each type of system that way. Group 1, you have the mayor-council system, Group 2, the commission system, Group 3, the council-manager system, and Group 4, special-purpose districts. Read and master your section, then figure out how you'll teach it to the rest of the class. Your group's presentation must include notes to share, a visual, and one other technique of your choice. I'm setting the timer for 30 minutes. It's up to you to liven up this material. Begin."

"I don't know whether to color my hair Autumn Gold or Sunshine Gold," said Alicia.

Cassie grabbed Jamie's hand. "Where did you get that sparkly nail polish?"

"I can't decide which dress to wear to my cousin's wedding." Jordan held up pictures from her pink and purple-striped smart phone.

"Girls in Group 1, get to work!"

Lindsey from Group 3 got out a jumbo pack of gum and threw pieces to students in other groups.

Someone in Group 4 must have passed gas. "God, Douglas, excuse yourself and check your underwear while you're at it," Michael complained, paging through a sports magazine.

"Time out," I yelled. "There hasn't been a lick of work accomplished so far. When you keep acting like fools, all you're doing is making me rich. I write down everything you say and use it for the book I'm writing called *School Stories*."

"Oh, please read us one," Dylan requested.

"Am I in it?" asked Sylvia.

"You're all in it. Just keep feeding me material for my book." I picked up my clipboard and walked from group to group, pretending to write down everything they said.

"We have pages 84–88 on the mayor-council system," said Lindsey, her group scurrying to open their texts.

"I'll read; Cassie, you take notes; and Jordan and Jamie, go get markers for the visual," said Alicia, setting aside Jordan's phone.

"Douglas and I will think up some review questions for the commission system," said Michael dropping his feet and magazine to the floor.

I put my clipboard in front of my face to hide my smirk, congratulating myself on a teaching technique I'd never divulge to them.

DAY 73
Being Cool

"We're not cool this quarter, Ms. Ball," Stewart informed me before class today.

He must have found out I reported him to Mrs. Stein, our dean of students. I suspected him of adding a nip to his sports drink in the plastic bottle he carries around with him. I told her I smelled alcohol, and his alternate euphoria and slumber added to my suspicion. The big bags of Doritos and popcorn he noisily munches on every morning in first bell, all the while talking to classmates over my lectures, did not help his cause.

"And what does it take to be cool with you, Stewart? Let you drink, eat, talk, and sleep in class? And when the quarter is over, give you an A?"

"That sounds cool," he grinned.

"Sorry, Stewart, I'm not cool, so you're right, we're not cool."

DAY 74
Letter to the Editor/ Let Teachers Assign Grades

If you want to explain the concept of socialism, compare it to the grading system in many public high schools: Everyone gets a diploma whether they earn it or not. You can explain communism by referring to school board policies that force teachers to award students a 50% for a skipped assignment.

Dawson's and White's articles on the "no-zero" policy merit further discussion. So far, the role of the teacher has been omitted. As a high school teacher with 26 years of experience, I happen to take my job seriously. My syllabus does not base an entire course on one grade. If an *Elizabeth* has a "mid-September lapse," I want to know why. If the lapse is legitimate, I will certainly allow her to make up assignments. Even if the lapse is not, I will encourage her to complete the work for partial credit. As White said, work is the priority.

I know of no teacher who enjoys giving zeroes; yet, it's an insult to my profession to be forced to give a student a 50% for work he did not do, has no intention of doing, and has no good excuse for not doing. This is a disservice to a student who receives a 60 or 70 on a project and sees *Elizabeth* receiving a 50 for nothing. It is a disservice to society sending graduates into the work force with no work ethic. A "no-zero" policy lowers academic standards to accommodate the laziest of students.

As Dawson stated, it doesn't take a genius to figure out that minimum effort will pass a class. Many schools are not excellent because excellence is not required. Administrators do not empower their two greatest resources, students and teachers. Students are capable of quality work, and teachers, who work directly with them, are capable of making decisions on their behalf. The Soviet system failed because competition, incentive, and individual rights were lacking. American schools could use a healthy shot of capitalism.

DAY 75
Parental Contact

I gave Eric a detention for disrupting class. On it I wrote: *Repeated calling out to another student across the room despite my several polite requests to keep quiet.* His mother phoned me and said I was picking on her son. "I don't have time to pick on anyone," I explained. "I have 120 students, lessons to prepare, grading to do, and the care of my elderly parents when I leave school. I didn't get up this morning with the intention of picking on Eric. His behavior hit me in the face and kept me from teaching my lesson. When he ignored my simple *please be quiet* I felt as though I were being picked on. Thank you for calling."

DAY 76
Indirect Democracy More Directly/ School News Article

Although we live in a democracy, 100 million voters all over the United States can't go to Washington D.C. and make decisions on health care, the federal budget, or military deployment. Instead, we elect congressmen to represent our position on these issues. Citizens choose 100 senators, two from each state, and 438 representatives, the number from each state depending on its population. 538 congressmen make up our indirect democracy. Direct voting on issues is possible only in small towns such as Madison, where all voters can decide on a school levy, or whether to build a new park or swimming pool.

Students in government class put names and faces to our 538 representatives. After choosing a congressman, they researched categories such as family and educational background, committee assignments, case work, and ability to get reelected. Students entered the information on a report card, and they got to grade their men and women based on performance.

D.J. Walters gave Senate Majority Leader Harry Reid an A+ for earning the respect of colleagues from both parties for his integrity and guts. Heidi Dawson gave Senator Lindsey Graham, the top vote getter in South Carolina history, an A+ for reelection. Tyler Harrod was impressed that Ohio's Senator Sherrod Brown graduated from Yale University, and gave him an A+ for educational background. Scott Brown, a former model, won the late Ted Kennedy's Senate seat in Massachusetts. Lori Smith suggested that his good looks may have helped the republican win in a traditionally democratic state. Reading, Ohio can boast of John Boehner. As speaker of the House, he is the third most powerful man in the U.S. Dave Miller gave him an A for athleticism because he was a linebacker for Moeller High School.

Students enjoyed researching political and personal information of a large and seemingly distant body of 538 congressmen. Through their report cards, they experienced our indirect democracy more directly.

DAY 77
Enemy Fire

My colleague Mrs. Keller and I looked at each other as we shut our doors after students rushing through after the bell had rung. Shouting and shoving, shirts out, they carried nothing in preparation for class. "This ought to be good," she said as we parted to face our classes.

"Get away from the windows and sit down," I yelled. "Take out your homework." I picked up my clipboard and walked through the rows. "Jeremy."

"Got it," he said. I stared down at his pitiful effort, but knew it would be better than most. I checked his box.

"Martin." There was nothing on his desk so I added an X to all his others. "Darrell."

"Somebody stole my book," he whined. I gave him an X and moved on. I'd already called his mother, kept him after class, organized his notebooks and folders, and coached him through a routine whereby he could get to class with all his materials."

"The first book is free," I announced for the 40th time. "The second book is $50. I have 120 students. I can't babysit everybody's stuff."

Desiree and Terrace got checks as usual. "Daniel, where's your work?"

"It's in my dad's car. Can I get credit for it tomorrow?"

"No, we're discussing it today."

Some discussion I had. Four of eighteen students had work—fourteen rounds of excuses, apathy, and disorganization. Desiree, Terrace, Jeremy, Trey and I reviewed the homework while the others were cooking up a good one.

"Who can name the five new weapons introduced during WWI?"

"Machine guns, flamethrowers, poison gas, large cannons, and tanks," answered Trey.

"Excellent." I turned to write them on the board and heard a heavy object hit the wall. I turned back to eighteen innocent faces. *Just my imagination. Keep moving through the lesson.* "The machine gun was the first truly automatic weapon. How many bullets did it fire per minute?"

Desiree raised her hand. "I read like 600 of them."

"Good. In the Battle of Verdun 8,000 men were killed in four hours. As I wrote *Verdun* on the board, I heard several more crashes against the wall. *Not my imagination.* I turned to eighteen innocent faces. Big grey rocks covered the floor.

The kids were hoping I'd get all upset, stop class, and waste time investigating. Instead, I said, "Open your books to page 331 and read to the end of the chapter. Jeremy, pass out these questions. I'll collect them tomorrow for a grade. I'll stand here on patrol. It's clear I can't turn my back and we can't have a nice discussion."

When the class ended, I picked up the rocks and put them in an envelope. "I've been here 26 years," I told the principal, "and never has anyone thrown rocks. What parents would want their children in this environment?"

He looked in the Manila envelope and said dismissively, "It looks like they got them from the playground."

Furious, I took my case to the dean of students who promised to investigate. After questioning reliable students, Mrs. Stein narrowed it down to Dion and Ashley. I wasn't surprised, since I caught Ashley throwing markers the day before.

For sympathy, I went to Mrs. Keller's room. "I've had paper wads, broken pencils and crayons, and pieces of granola spat and thrown at me, but rocks take it to a whole new level."

"It's the end of the month," she said. "Let's celebrate." I went for the November page of my large desk calendar. We each took a side and with much pomp and satisfaction said, "One, two, three, rip!"

"Three months down and six to go." I said.

The next day I retreated to the trenches in the back of the room to protect myself from enemy fire. I could see everyone, but they couldn't see me or where I was looking. Occasionally I moved from Dion's to Ashley's desk and stood there for several minutes. I taught like this for a week. Meanwhile Mrs. Stein searched their lockers and rearranged things so they knew they were under investigation. They finally got the message I knew who threw the rocks, and that, as far as war strategy was concerned, I was General Pershing calling all the shots.

DAY **78**
Definition of Success

Today I didn't hit anyone or direct profanity at anyone. Some days by the end of the day, that's all I've accomplished. I know those are pretty low standards, but the way the day went, that was success enough. That means I still have a job, and who knows what headway I'll make tomorrow.

DAY 79
Misery Loves Company

If it weren't for other teachers, I'd go insane. I receive a great amount
of reassurance listening to their stories, and realize I'm not the only one
experiencing this phenomenon called *school kids' behavior*. Mainly we stand
alone, one teacher against 25 kids for six periods a day; but lunchtime is our
opportunity for solidarity. The matter of fact account of Mrs. Carson, veteran
fifth grade teacher, captivated us in the teachers' lounge today.

"Seth cried for two hours again this morning," related Mrs. Carson. Seth
is the class hypochondriac who either doesn't come to school, or sits and cries
for his mother imagining all sorts of ailments. "Today he had chest pains. I
told him I had a sinus headache and my back hurt, but I still came to school.
He kept on crying. I told him to go sit down, and when he starts to turn blue
to let me know."

Eric, the delinquent of the sixth grade, goes to Mrs. Carson's class
for reading each day. His black unkempt hair matches his noncompliance.
"I excused Eric to go to the restroom this morning," she said. "When he
returned, he started telling me about Cody. From bits and pieces of what Eric
was saying, I realized this couldn't be discussed in the classroom. I took Eric
out into the hall and he said, 'Cody was in the bathroom with his pants down
humping the wall.' Eric is a scoundrel, but he doesn't lie, so I kept listening
when he said, 'Then when I went in the hall to get a drink, Cody mooned me.'"
Mrs. Carson continued on, "I got a referral form and tried to write down what
Eric reported. I wasn't sure if *humping* was spelled with one *p* or two. I was
so flustered I went across the hall to Miss Carpenter's room and asked her. I

didn't want to make a spelling error on the referral. She wasn't sure if *hump* is a verb too or only a noun. We looked it up and it's a verb, so we agreed on one p. By the way, Cody is the student I was telling you about who brought the pornographic video to school, called *Consenting Adults*. He asked if the class could watch it during indoor recess."

We crumbled our brown paper bags when lunch ended, feeling more nourished from Mrs. Carson's stories than from the food we ate.

DAY 80
No Gifts Please

In the middle of December my students start asking me what I want for Christmas. "Please don't get me anything," I beg, "I have everything I need at home. The best present you can give me is to do your homework. I love good grades." Of course no one ever listens to me. The day before Christmas break the homework isn't done, and the gifts pile on my desk. I expect the usual mugs, candles, and ornaments from the Dollar Store, but some gifts have taken me aback.

Last year, a *World Book Encyclopedia* won 2nd place for all time astonishing gifts. The lone Volume D, 1967, had toddler scribble on the pages, food and drink stains, and a strong smell of mildew. I didn't know how to thank Ryan when he handed it to me. This year, Rhonda's gift topped his. Her round eyes were on me as I opened the Santa Claus wrap to a yellowed glass cupid figurine with a chipped wing. It hung on a tarnished chain, and it tipped sideways from the bent pole and dusty stand. "It's beautiful, I love it, thank you, Rhonda." I hoped she didn't notice the bewilderment in my voice.

Next, I had to deal with the homemade cookies, cakes, and candy. Everyone wanted me to try theirs right away. I pictured the kitchens where these goodies came from—cats walking on the counters, kids licking batter from their fingers, petting their dogs, and then dropping globs of dough onto the cookie sheets. Destiny brought me burnt crumpled brownies in a rusty pan. My stomach flipped when Stephanie shoved her buckeyes in my face. "Me and my sister made these last night. Have one now." I'm sure I wasn't imagining traces of hair rolled into the peanut butter part and fingerprints all over the lopsided balls.

"I'll take them to lunch with me," I promised, "and save the rest for home." In the refuge of the teachers' lounge, I threw the delicacies away. "They were delicious," I told the kids later. "I tried a little of each."

When the kids were gone that afternoon, I gathered the good will and left a note for the custodians. *Please take or pitch.* Exhausted from faking pleasure and appreciation, I thought, *why couldn't they just do their homework?*

DAY 81
More Bullshit

The Ohio State Department of Education is at it again. They've come out with three new mandates to torment teachers and underachieving schools—new school ratings, teacher evaluations tied to student performance, and Common Core standards and tests. The new school ratings are A,B,C,D, and F, instead of Excellent with Distinction, Excellent, Continuous Improvement, Academic Watch, and Academic Emergency.

Big whoop! So Wyoming, Indian Hill, and Mariemont get *As* instead of Excellent with Distinction, and the inner city schools get *Ds* and *Fs* instead of Academic Watch and Emergency. The state says the letter grades are easier for the public to understand. Understand what—affluence and educated parents produce higher student achievement, and poverty and uneducated parents produce lower achievement? Labels or letters, we know that anyway.

In addition, teacher hiring, firing, promotion, and pay will be tied to student growth, but "experts" have not explained how that will work in all subjects and grade levels. How can growth be measured in the relatively few months one teacher is with one class of students? Theoretically, it's easy in the standardized tested subjects and grades. Teacher performance is based on test results. In the non-tested subjects such as art and foreign language, the teacher is supposed to make up his own "Student Learning Objectives" and tests, and produce data to show student growth. Teachers may spend countless hours on this requirement, taking the focus away from their students and creative and engaging lessons. In fear of losing their jobs or taking a salary reduction, what's to prevent teachers from making up easy tests and teaching to those tests in the classroom?

Since around 1990 the state has mandated the Proficiency Test, the Ohio Achievement Test, the Ohio Graduation Test, and now the Common Core Test. The results have not changed. Certain schools are rated higher and certain schools are rated lower according to income and parents. We don't need different tests, new labels, or threatening teacher evaluations to tell us that.

In a recent column, Walter Williams wrote: "Whether a student is black or white, poor or rich, there are some minimum requirements that must be met to do well in school. Someone must make the student do his homework, see to it he gets a good night's sleep, fix a breakfast, make sure he gets to school on time and make sure he respects and obeys his teachers. Which can be achieved by politicians?"

It's the responsibility of education programs in the universities to train and send good teachers into the schools and the responsibility of parents to send their children to school ready to learn. The Ohio Department of Education does not need to micromanage schools. The real "experts" should be university professors, experienced teachers, and parents.

DAY 82
The Good Old Days

Students used to go to school worrying about what kind of mood their teacher would be in that day. Now teachers go to school worrying about what kind of mood their students will be in that day.

DAY 83
Parental Support

There's no better place to go after a bad day at school than to my parents' house for dinner. I get a great meal, conversation that revolves around me, and guaranteed love and support.

"How did it go today?" asked Mom.

"Terrible, the kids are awful," I replied, feeling free to dump the day's frustrations on the kitchen table.

"What do they do?" asked Dad.

"They talk while I'm trying to teach. When I politely ask them to be quiet, they give me a dirty look as if I'm the one who's doing something wrong. Then they continue talking."

"What do you do then?" Mom asked.

"After about the fifth request to be quiet, I tell them to go sit in the hallway. Then they throw a tantrum. They call me a MF, throw their books and notebooks on the floor, hurl their chairs against the wall, and stomp out yelling, "I hate this school!"

"Why don't you send them to the office instead of the hallway?" asked Dad.

"Because the principal sends them right back to the room. They brag in front of the others that no one did anything."

"You mean there's no consequence for that type of behavior?" asked Mom.

"They might get a detention, but they skip it and no one in authority follows up."

"It sounds like your school needs an effective discipline program," said Dad.

"That's impossible," I explained. "The superintendent has mandated against suspensions and expulsions. They make the district look bad. Administrators don't want to go to court when parents challenge their decisions, and our district needs to get the attendance indicator for the school report card that is published in the newspaper. If the district looks bad, residents won't vote for the school levy."

"Partly, the principal's hands are tied," said Dad.

"Yes, and partly, no one will take a courageous stand for what is right," I said. "The school cowers in front of parents. I've been in a lot of schools and I've never yet seen a strong principal like the one in the movie *Lean on Me*. That man cleaned the whole school out."

"All the students can't be acting like that," said Dad.

"No, but there are one or two each class period. It upsets me and I lose my train of thought and my lesson is less effective for the ones behaving."

"I'd knock them out," said Mom.

"Mom, you don't lay a finger on kids anymore. I'd get fired. If you even lightly put your hand on their arm, they jerk away and yell, 'You can't touch me!'"

"They sure know their rights and what teachers can't do, but they don't know their lessons," said Dad. "This all started when prayer was taken out of the public schools."

"When I was in school," said Mom, "we couldn't even smile. I can still hear Sister Mary Leonardo scolding me, 'Wipe that silly grin off your face, Miss Eggleston.'"

"Yeah," said Dad. "One day Father Odo walked down my row and hit me on the head. I was stunned and couldn't figure out what I was doing wrong. I was an honor student and played football and everything."

"When I used to wait on kids in the shoe store," said Mom, "I'd pinch their toes if they acted up."

"I don't have that freedom," I said.

"Oh honey, do the best you can," said Dad. "Remember, it's not you. It's their home-life and it's society."

Mom got up to clear the table while I loaded the dishwasher. "Just get your paycheck," she said.

Dad stayed seated drinking his tea, pondering how to fix my problem.

DAY 84
Saved by Mr. Slate

I am such a threat to 6th graders, that today the local branch of Health and Human Services was called in to investigate me. I told Keith I was going to kill him when he wouldn't keep quiet during practice for our elementary Christmas concert. Then I dragged Ethan from under a group of desks when he refused to get up off of the floor. Keith and Ethan happened to be cousins. Their mothers got together and accused me of child abuse. The evidence was a slight rug burn near Ethan's elbow when I got him off of the floor. The mothers thought they could report me, sue, and make some money.

I had to answer questions in a small meeting room by the office with Mr. Slate, the principal, by my side. "I meant nothing by *kill*," I told the representative. "We used the word as a hyperbole around our house. 'I am going to kill you,' my sisters and I would jokingly say to each other when we were kids." As for the rug burn, I explained that I asked Ethan five times to please get off of the floor. When he kept ignoring me, I got him up myself. His safety was my main concern. I feared he would be stabbed with the leg of a chair that another student was rocking back and forth on.

"Mrs. Ball has been a highly qualified teacher here for over twenty years and I'm sure she had the boys' best interest in mind," added Mr. Slate.

In preparation for the meeting, I tried to look as harmless as possible. I wore a long skirt and dowdy blouse and pulled my hair back into a barrette. Surprisingly, the representative wasn't on the offense and didn't seem to doubt my credibility; and with Mr. Slate to back me up, nothing came from the accusations.

"Whatever you do," he said after the meeting, "don't lay a hand on a student and never make any references to violence. People are so sensitive now days. Someone is always waiting for you to say and do the wrong thing. You have to be on guard at all times. You know you mean no harm but others don't assume that same good will."

After that scare I realized I'm always on display in the classroom and I'd better treat it as a stage. Every remark and action in front of students must be monitored. *Kill* is out of my vocabulary and, the next time, Ethan can stay on the floor.

DAY 85
Back When I Was in School

"Ms. Ball, you've got to watch *Duck Dynasty*," interrupted Sylvia right in the middle of French class.

"What's *Duck Dynasty* and what does it have to do with –ir verbs?" I was fully annoyed.

"It's this TV show," she said. "How do you say *Duck Dynasty* in French?"

I wrote *Dynastie du Canard* on the board. "*Voila*, Sylvia, now let's get back to our verb endings."

I don't watch TV and I've never heard of *Duck Dynasty*. Current programs are insipid as I fondly recall *Ben Casey*, *Ed Sullivan*, and *Bonanza*. I'm out of touch with the taste of today's youth.

And speaking of taste, I hate the way kids think they need to eat and drink in the classroom all day. This morning, before I could protest, Stewart set up a pancake breakfast in homeroom. After first bell, syrup covered his desk. I didn't see it until the next occupant squealed in disgust, her arm stuck in Stewart's mess. All morning kids snack on pop and chips, and in the afternoon, candy and gum. Picking up wrappers, crumbs, and empty bottles at day's end, I'm more janitor than teacher.

When I was in school, we ate breakfast at home, ate lunch in the cafeteria, and didn't eat again until we got home. There was a concept called delayed gratification. We ate only at mealtimes except for a snack after school.

And how did I survive the day without a cell phone, unable to text my mom or friends? I never thought of my mom, and my friends were all in school with me anyway.

Today at 10:15 I yelled at Maya in third bell. At 10:25 her mother was at my door yelling at me for yelling at Maya. My mom would be the last person I'd contact if I got in trouble. She'd yell at me worse than the teacher and hit me on top of it. And how did I get through the halls without an iPod hanging from my ears and a boyfriend at my side?

I won't say I walked seven miles to school in the snow, but I never told a teacher I couldn't do my work because I didn't have a pencil. I was never sent to the office for disrespect, and no one rewarded me for perfect attendance or good grades. After *Ben Casey* I went to bed and wasn't up all night on Facebook or Twitter.

"Mrs. Ball," whined Sylvia. "Will you please *print* the French for *Duck Dynasty?* I can't read cursive."

DAY 86
SLOs

First thing this morning, I passed out a pretest to my senior government students. The state is requiring documentation of student growth, so we teachers have to give a pretest at the beginning of the year and the same test at the end to show that students have attained a year's worth of growth in a particular subject. If data shows little or no growth, teachers get a poor evaluation and a possible cut in pay, promotion denial, or even dismissal. Along with our data, we have to submit Student Learning Objectives (SLOs) relating to the new Common Core Standards designed to promote critical thinking and problem solving skills. It makes no sense because what's to prevent a teacher from giving a difficult pretest, then feeding that material to the class all year? Of course the students will show growth.

Annoyed with the new requirements, I gave the papers to the first student in each row to pass back. I had a cool Walter Williams article I wanted to work on that day instead of the pretest. As I wrote test directions on the board, I heard a ruckus in Shaq's row. "Shaq won't pass the papers back," said Robby. Shaq was hiding his row's papers under his book and Robby was trying to get to one. They started shoving each other.

"Shaq, pass the papers back," I said.

"What? What you talkin' about?" he said looking at me blankly as though I were a fool.

Robby wrestled the papers from under Shaq's book and passed them to the others. The remaining one for Shaq was wrinkled. "I want a new paper," he demanded. "I ain't writin' on this one."

"Since you caused the problem, that's your paper," I said. "Write on it or take a zero."

The class started the test and I noticed Shaq looking at his phone under his desk. "Shaq please put your phone in your pocket." I was trying to defuse his behavior and avoid sending anyone to the office. Five minutes later I lost it when Shaq had his phone back out. "Go to the office," I said.

"What you mean? I ain't doin' nothin'."

"Out," I yelled.

"No," he said.

I turned around and pressed the call button below the intercom. "Yes," answered the secretary.

"Mrs. Lewis, please send Officer Roush to remove a student from my room."

Shaq scrambled from his desk and out the door. I got a referral form and checked *disruption, defiance, insubordination,* and wrote a description of what had transpired.

After class I was certain what my SLOs would be and hurried to write them while they were fresh in my mind.

1. The student will pass back papers to others in his row as directed by the teacher.

2. The student will put his phone away during a test as directed.

3. The student will leave the room for disruption when directed by the teacher.

This is to inform the state that there will be no critical thinking or problem solving skills demonstrated by students until these minimum requirements have been met.

DAY 87
Medley

My daughter PJ is a teacher, too. Only she has a PhD and teaches college chemistry. She is certified to teach high school, but after her student teaching she decided no way. "I'm not going to spend the day telling kids to take off their hats and put away their iPods," she said.

On Friday evenings my husband Jim and I often have dinner with our daughter and niece, a teacher also. This evening, Friday the 13th, Jim needed several beers to endure our three school stories during dinner.

PJ went first. "In lab today I asked this guy to describe what the product of his experiment looked like. 'Cum,' he said. 'Ew,' two girls at his table gasped, and the other guy gave a snide laugh. I just walked away."

"Gross," I said, "I'd rather deal with the hats and iPods."

My niece Amy teaches 2nd grade in a Montessori school. "Five times this morning, a kid spilled a container of colored pencils all over the floor and made a scene picking them up. The first time was an accident and the next four were on purpose. I kept him in from recess and handed him the tray of pencils. 'Spill the pencils,' I said. 'Now pick them up.' 'Again, spill the pencils!' 'Now pick them up!' He started to cry after the fourth time. 'Funny,' I said, 'this morning you seemed to enjoy what you were doing and now you don't. What's different? Again, spill the pencils. Now pick them up…'"

"That's brilliant," I said.

As for me, today was picture day. The seniors were first to be called to the auditorium during first bell. At the beginning of third bell, there was a call for anyone who hadn't yet had his picture taken. Tony came late to school so I let him go. Twenty minutes elapsed and Tony hadn't returned to class. I went to the auditorium to check on him and they said he left fifteen minutes ago. Furious, I returned to my room and wrote a cut slip on him. He showed up at the end of the bell as though nothing happened.

"You have an office referral for skipping class," I said. "You should've been gone only five minutes."

"Oh, I can get you a note from coach," he said. Being a football player gave him a sense of entitlement.

"I don't want any note from any coach," I replied. "You were to return to class immediately after your picture. You missed current events along with chapter 12 test, to add to chapter 11 test you missed last week."

"But coach will…"

"I don't care about coach! I'm not accepting any note from any coach! Now go to your next class."

My husband got up to pay the bill not having enjoyed the stories as much as PJ, Amy and I. He missed talking sports with his brother who usually joins us.

Cum, colored pencils, or coach—college, elementary, or high school—we three agreed there's no easy way for a teacher to make a living.

DAY 88
Beatles or Founding Fathers?

Troublesome news for government teachers has been appearing in news articles over the past several years. Journalists such as Walter Williams, Kathleen Parker, and Leonard Pitts write that history and government are students' worst subjects and that Americans are losing their memory.

One survey reported that 98% of students could identify Bevis and Butt-Head, but only 34% knew that George Washington was the general at Yorktown. A cartoon showed a busload of students on a field trip to Mt. Rushmore. They remarked, "Like, I knew they were important, but I had no idea the Beatles were *that* big!"

Determined my government students wouldn't make such foolish blunders, I gave them a sample naturalization test issued by the U.S. Citizenship and Immigration Services. They had to answer 35 questions on American history, geography, and government and score 60% or higher to pass.

I have a lot of work to do between now and June when these graduates enter society as voting adults. Of the 27 students tested, only 10 would receive a certificate of naturalization. To the question, *Name one of two of the longest rivers in the U.S.*, one student answered *The Nile*.

DAY 89
Oasis

I can't believe my good fortune in my honors senior government class. I can finish a sentence without getting cut off. Actually, I can finish a whole thought. Moreover, I can finish a whole lesson without pleading *Please be quiet* five times, then *Be quiet* five times, then finally *Shut up!* I can't believe I don't have to send anyone to the office.

I don't know how to act in a room full of kids with their eyes on me while I'm talking—Samantha, Mary, Tevin, Brinton, and Kayla. Everyone is quiet and listening to me. Then I listen to the sounds of pens and pencils scratching in notebooks, pages turning in textbooks, a muffled cough, and a soft sneeze. "Where did you find number 12?" Kayla whispers to Sam. Eyes on my own work, I hear the grind of the pencil sharpener, the click of the keyboard, the rustle of papers placed neatly on my desk. The bell rings. The bell? Is class over already?

DAY 90
Behind the Scenes

Zippy wasn't in my second bell class, but I saw her later in the hall. "Zippy, where were you this morning?" I asked.

"My clothes were in the dryer," she explained.

"Glad you're here now," I replied eyeing her faded pink polo and khaki pants. Incredulous, I wondered if her answer was evidence of not caring, a dysfunctional home life, poverty, or some of each. I wanted to shake her and say, *You mean you didn't realize you needed school clothes before this morning?* Instead I said, "Stop by my room and get your assignment before the end of the day."

"Okay," she said. By her distracted gaze I knew she wouldn't come and that missing my class was not a big part of her life.

DAY 91
Jock Itch

I know it's the end of the second quarter because the jocks come into my room circling and sniffing around my desk. Antwan, Seth and Jake acknowledge my existence for the first time all year, "Hey Ms. Ball, what's up?"

"Not your grades." I continue working. They sit on the edge of the desks in front of mine, grin and dangle their legs. "Uh, could we see them at least?"

"There's nothing to see. You all have Fs."

They try and play *best friend* with me. "Aw, Ms. Ball, we need to be eligible for basketball." They think I'm so thrilled by their presence that I'm simply going to walk back to the computer and change their Fs to Ds.

"You should have thought of that six weeks ago when your heads were on the desk and you mumbled profanity at me when I asked for your work."

"We're sorry, Ms. Ball. Coach wants to know our grades."

I take my time going to the computer to print them out. "Seth, you have a 34% for the quarter. My class is from 10:45 to 11:30. I notice you get to school most days around 11:30 just in time to take your girlfriend to the cafeteria. I hand Antwan his report. He gasps at his 16% average. "You have spent most of the quarter in the In School Discipline Room. It's impossible to watch slides and take notes from there." I turn to Jake. "When I called your house to set up a conference with your parents, you disguised your voice and said that I had the wrong number and that I had reached Jake's Pizza Parlor."

"How'd you know about that?" he said staring at his 28%.

They saw I wasn't playing *best friend* and that I wasn't as impressed with them as the young ladies in school. "Uh, could you give us some make up work?"

"You can't do a quarter's worth of work in one day. Tomorrow is Friday and grades are due."

"Could you give us a chance? We gotta be eligible for basketball."

I go to the file cabinet and get out assignments on political action groups, Gandhi, imperialism, and WWI. It's a waste of time. I know they won't do all this work, but I throw the responsibility back on them. I can't let anyone say I didn't let them try. I hand them ten papers apiece. "Could you give us until Tuesday?"

"No, you have to go by the school's deadline. I have to send my grades by 3:00 tomorrow, at which time I'm leaving for the golf course. You're not the only ones who play sports."

"Aw man." They roll their papers up, head for the door, and pause. Realizing there's nothing more to get from me, they leave, heads drooping in front of them and pants drooping behind.

DAY 92
A Hell of a Start

Wanyé was back in class after a three day suspension. That followed a previous five day suspension. How he got a lesser punishment was beyond me. According to the school's discipline policy, punishments are supposed to increase with each infraction, going from a one day, to a three day, to a five day, to a ten day suspension, then expulsion. But it's basketball season and he's one of the starters so apparently the rules don't apply to athletes.

I dragged myself to school this morning with a sore throat and headache. I wasn't happy to see Wanyé, (Wan-yeah). I called him Wayne the first day of school and was immediately reprimanded. I looked again at the roster and indeed the n preceded the y. At 6'2", 230 pounds, his physical presence is noticeable enough. And with his return today, the noise level in the room increased tenfold. Nevertheless, I was determined to keep calm.

I passed out the chapter 6 test that I'd been warning the kids about for the last three days. "Remember," I said, "you can use anything you wrote in your own notebook, but you can't open your text."

"I didn't know about any test," growled Wanyé. "I ain't takin' it."

To myself I said, *Of course you didn't know about it, Jerk, you got yourself suspended.* To him I said, "Wanyé, you can read chapter 6 during this bell and copy the study notes I left on the board. You can take the test tomorrow."

"I ain't takin it tomorrow, I'm takin' it Friday," he retorted.

"Wanyé, you have this whole bell to prepare. I'm not even obligated to allow you a make-up day since you were suspended and not sick. You can take it now or tomorrow, that's it."

"I ain't doing nothin' today," he said, flinging his books, notebooks, and folders on the floor and laying his head on his desk.

"Enough," I said, "go to the office if you're not going to follow directions."

School started at 8. I looked up at the clock. It was 8:05. After a suspension, Wanyé lasted five minutes.

He started to leave when his buddy Tony got up and piped in, "Don't get him in trouble. He ain't doin' nothin'."

"That's just the point," I said. "Mind your own business, Tony, take your headphones off, and begin your test."

Tony came toward me saying, "You can't send him to the office, he'll get suspended again. We got a game tonight." He got in my face and kept giving me orders.

"Shut up," I yelled. "Shut up!"

I must have been formidable because Tony sat down and Wanyé left for the office. Astounded I had silenced the room and that the kids began working, I steadied myself at my desk. Delirious with a pounding headache and throat on fire, I thought, *What a way to start the day. Five more bells and 100 more students to go.*

DAY 93
No Admittance

Tony just made the opening bell, a McDonald's bag in hand. "Put that away," I said, "class begins at 8, not breakfast."

He took the bag into the hall, found a comfortable chair from the opposite room, and had his Egg McMuffin, hash browns, and fruit smoothie. I closed my door, took attendance, and started class. Fifteen minutes later Tony swaggered into the room. "Go to the office and check in. I counted you absent."

"But I was here on time. You seen me." He raised his hands as though I were completely out of my mind.

"You weren't in your seat ready for class. Go get a late pass and return minus the sunglasses and headphones."

"Ms. Ball, why you playin' him?" Shaq butted in. "He was here at 8."

"I don't need any help with classroom management, Shaq."

"Tony, go to the office or I'm calling Officer Reed."

"You're fucking geeking," he replied.

"And you're out of here," I retorted pressing the call button.

DAY 94
Zen for the Classroom

I threw a tantrum at Maya. I yelled so loud my throat hurt. I was so shook up I had to take a walk after school in the cold rain. I couldn't believe that after 25 years in the classroom and with my knowledge of Zen practices I still let kids get to me like that.

Maya was copying Katie's English papers during government class. I noticed them spread all over her desk, but decided not to react. I simply walked back to her and whispered to put the English away. I had every right to take it. One of my classroom rules is *government only during government*. I couldn't begin to deal with the cheating issue. Don't take yourself too seriously, I reminded myself.

Pleased with my conscious Presence, I resumed teaching. Maya got the English out again and resumed copying. "Collecting taxes is a concurrent power," I said walking back and taking the papers from her. "Callie, please stop your private conversation with Tyler."

"Man, ain't she nasty," muttered Maya to the kids around her.

"Maya, that's enough. Go to the office," I said.

"You're lame," she cried, slamming her books down and grabbing her huge purse. "Go ahead and write me up." All the kids laughed.

Knowing she'd be back for her English, I expected her after school, but pretended to look surprised to see her. "Yes, Maya?"

"I need those papers."

"You have no right to anything but government work in my room," I said. "Besides, I asked you once to put them away."

"No you didn't."

At that point I became, in Zen language, *unconscious.* "Yes I did," I screamed. "And you called me *nasty* when I corrected Callie. That had nothing to do with you."

"No I didn't."

"Yes you did," I screamed. "This school doesn't hire deaf teachers. And I suppose you didn't call me *lame.* I suppose you don't call me Mrs. *Balls* every day. I suppose you don't hang all over Jonathan when I'm trying to start class and call him your *baby* and your *husband.* And I'm sick and tired of the nicknames you use in here: *Chocolate Deluxe* for yourself, *Butterscotch, Peanut Butter,* and *Angel Food* for your friends. And I've seen your act in the library sixth bell wasting your study hall and driving Miss Amyx crazy. Now, I'll show you *nasty* and *lame.*" I ripped up the English papers and threw them into the garbage can.

"Hey, them are for Mrs. Keller's class," she cried.

"Go see if she'll give you another set. Maybe you're a model student for her." Maya glared at me and she did not budge. "And now, Miss Cake Mix Queen, get out of my room. I have work to do."

The next day Maya did not open her mouth in government. It's a good thing because I was still holding a grudge. If she whispered or even breathed I'd kick her out. After class she came up to my desk. "I apologize for how I been actin' all year."

I was astonished. Somehow my unprofessionalism worked. "I accept," I said. "Remember, government only in government."

"Yes, Ma'am."

I'm writing a teaching manual called *Zen for the Classroom.* The five best practices for managing students are: 1. *Don't react* 2. *Stay conscious* 3. *Be present* 4. *Redirect quietly* and 5. *Don't take yourself too seriously.* And when those don't work, throw a tantrum!

DAY 95
Answers May Vary

Over the years the kids have educated me on the many ways to cheat. I am grateful for this knowledge since I've never cheated in school myself. Cheating was not part of the culture at my private Catholic school run by nuns in the 1950s. Now, cheating on homework, tests, and reports is common practice. "It would serve you better to use your ingenuity for legal purposes," I tell them.

The mildest form is the *Cheat Sheet*, an index card with little writing hidden in sleeves or under desks. I call it mild since the answers are in the kid's own writing and show some interaction with the material.

Another technique, *Roaming Eyes* during a test, is fairly easy to control. I can spread the desks out and face them at the windows and walls.

A higher level of severity is what the kids call *Working Together*. One student has another's paper on his desk and copies straight from it. They are so desensitized to cheating that they do it right in front of me. When I tell them that neither will get credit they become indignant. "You said we could work together." I try and explain that working and copying are not the same.

A rather clever way to cheat is called *Name Switching*. Someone takes a friend's paper, scratches out his name and writes his own. I caught a sixth period student with work from fourth. I'd know Briana's big loopy handwriting anywhere, but her name was scratched out and replaced by Shanika. Briana did not understand why she did not get credit for work that she did. I told her to look up the word *accomplice* in the dictionary.

Plagiarism falls into a more serious category. For one assignment the students were to interview a Vietnam veteran and give a report to the class.

Tommy got up and started his report. Supposedly he interviewed his uncle who served in Vietnam. Then something he said caught my attention. His uncle had a PhD and taught political science at Stanford University. Now wait a minute. Few students in this school have relatives with any college degree much less a PhD. For that matter, high school diplomas are rare in this environment. Come to think of it, the sentence structure was much too sophisticated even if this fairly bright student had put effort into the report. Later, I Googled some of Tommy's phrases and they took me right to the Stanford University professor's account of his service in Vietnam.

Plagiarism is stealing words, but the most severe form of cheating is *Stealing a Teacher's Manual*. My *Government Alive* manual disappeared in September. I looked everywhere in the room for it. It must have amused whoever stole it to watch me slamming my desk and file cabinet drawers open and shut a million times. I suspected Monica who had a history of theft but I couldn't prove anything. I searched her locker and the lockers of most of the other kids in the class but found only dirty socks and sticky Hostess Cupcake wrappers. After a week I ordered another manual and put the incident out of my mind.

One afternoon in February I was sitting at my dining room table grading a stack of tests. My lost manual jumped right out of three students' papers. They got all of the multiple choices right, unlikely based on their past performances, and their short answers were suspicious with a word or phrase adjusted here and there. One girl didn't have enough sense to adjust the most sophisticated phrase in the whole answer key. She said the senator's speech had a "liberal bias." Then on the open-ended question my three suspects gave themselves away. They all wrote, *Student answers may vary. Students should provide an explanation that supports their answer to the survey question.* I rejoiced. Now I've nailed them. Surely I'd get my manual back.

The next day to outsmart them, I went through their lockers but found nothing. When I confronted them after class, all three said they copied off of each other but no one knew anything about the manual. "Someone had to use the answer key," I said. "*Student answers may vary* only appears in a teaching manual. It means you make up your own answer and don't copy." They argued with me, accused me of trying to fail them, and said they were getting their moms into the school after me.

I took the matter to the principal but nothing came of it. The only thing I could do was to have all work completed in class right before my eyes. It slowed down progress considerably. I also have made sure to maintain a giant snippy attitude with that class. Most of the kids know who took my manual, but no one has stepped forward. Whenever they ask me for a favor or if I'm going to their graduation I say, "As soon as my manual turns up. Teacher answers may vary."

DAY 96
TGIF

Today I got to school a little earlier than usual to search Donovan's locker. My seating chart and homework log were taken off my desk. Alyssa, whom I trust, told me Donovan slipped them in her notebook when my back was turned. I wanted so much to prove she took them but I found nothing. I guess she threw the evidence away. She's smart and sneaky. I can't stand her. I wanted to get her suspended. Stealing teacher records is no small offense. What's the matter with me? I'm the adult. It's not professional to dislike students. It served me right for not finding anything. I wasn't as smug as I thought I would be starting off my Friday.

Seniors in my first bell didn't do their homework. I was in front of the class busting my ass trying to teach it to them. Notebook in one hand, dry erase marker in the other, I was explaining and writing on the board. Mike cut in, "Do you have a Band-Aid?" I stopped and looked at him as though he were crazy. Then I looked from one of my hands to the other. "Yes, in my spare time I'll put all this down and walk over to my desk and get one out." I wanted to say, *What the hell are you thinking, you idiot?*

"I was just asking," he said.

At lunchtime a freshman girl, Desiree, walked right into the teachers' lounge and put money into the pop machine. "Are you getting that for a teacher?" I asked.

"No," she said. "Deion told me to get it for him."

"Deion? Give me that and get out of here." I took the 16 oz. Mountain Dew from her.

My colleague John and I looked at each other incredulously. "Can you believe how bold these kids are?" he said.

On the way to my room, Deion stopped me in the hall. "You'd better give me my pop or my money back," he said.

"You'd better get to class," I replied.

During fifth bell the freshmen were throwing rocks again. The floor was covered with them. Whenever I turned my back or moved somewhere else, they took their chance. Finally, I had to stand in the back of the room and police everyone. *Hell of a way to teach*, I thought.

I spent my free bell in the assistant principal's office planning a strategy to catch the rock throwers. I was sure Donovan and Deion were in on it.

I contained my seventh period kids for fifty minutes with current events and slides on the New Deal. Three minutes remained until the final bell of the day. As I congratulated myself on a job well done, Darrell and Daniel got up and started taunting and pushing each other. Three minutes left on a Friday afternoon, and a fight topped off the workweek. The resource officer came and removed the two boys.

As I sat down to write their referrals, Deion came back demanding his pop or money. "No way," I said. "One, students aren't allowed in the teachers' lounge, and two, students can't have drinks in the classroom. But while you're here, you can pick up the rocks you threw on the floor earlier." He stormed away muttering he's going to bring his mother in here on me. "Oh good," I called, "I've been trying to reach her for days." I crossed Friday off of my desk calendar and Deion's mom off of my to-do list and left for the weekend.

DAY 97
Babysitting

This school is blessed or cursed with Mrs. Hicks depending on your goals in education. The kids love to make fun of her and play tricks on her. At 5'6", 200 pounds she's a wide target. She wears knit tops over full calf-length skirts and stacked heel pumps looking several sizes too small. She cuts her salt and pepper hair in a Dutch girl style and her unevenly applied lipstick always makes it to her teeth.

I hear her teaching isn't any more modernized than her appearance. One day she fell asleep in her chair. The kids put a condom on her head and took a picture of her with their cell phones. "Hey Dear, did you hear what happened to me second bell?" I'm nice to Mrs. Hicks so she always comes to my room for sympathy, folded arms resting across her belly. Of course I heard what happened. Her language arts class comes to me third bell. I played dumb.

"Yeah, Lynsey was telling me something, but I cut her off to get class started."

"I was showing a movie and I dozed off for a few minutes. I'm on this allergy medicine and it makes me drowsy. That Carter girl took a picture of me, and I'm sure it was that smart ass Beardsley who put the condom on my head. She took her phone to Mr. Howard and he wrote me up and put it in my file."

"Oh brother," I said. "The kids should be written up. What are they doing with cell phones and condoms anyway?" Poor Mrs. Hicks, I try to side with her.

"It's not like I wasn't teaching. I was showing a movie and the kids had a worksheet with questions to answer."

"Don't worry. That class is out of control. I have problems with them too."

"Thanks for listening, Dear. Just wanted to let you know. Take care, Dear. I'm going to my room now and grade papers."

A few days later the kids were all stirred up coming to my room from Hicks'. I heard them saying she threw up in the garbage can during class. I dismissed the chatter having my own classroom management problems to worry about. When I was leaving for the day, I made my usual trip to the teachers' lounge. Hicks came out of the back room and cornered me. "Did you hear what happened to me today?"

"The kids said something about you being sick," I said.

"I was coming out of the Y by my house this morning, I have an aerobics class at 6 a.m., and I threw up in the parking lot. Then on the way in here, I got sick on myself in the car. See?" Her top had a big messy stain on the front. She kept walking toward me and I kept backing away. "Then I got sick again second bell in front of the kids. I've been lying back here on the couch ever since. Howard had to get me a sub. I finally feel stable enough to drive myself home. I think I had a reaction to that pain medicine I took last night."

"I hope you make it home okay," I said holding my breath and backing out the door.

Everyone is used to Mrs. Hicks. We accept her with a *roll your eyes and grin* kind of attitude. Everyone, that is, except the principal. "You know, Dear," she told me one afternoon, "Howard's out to get me. Ever since that cell phone thing, he's been watching me. This morning he walked by my room. He put a note in my mail box that said, *Head on desk, consider this a reprimand.* I was just stretching my back from my workout this morning. Then he tells me the OGT reading scores are so low he might not renew my contract next year. You know what kind of a day it's been? Let me put it this way. If it were raining dicks, I'd reach out and grab a tit. Anyway, Dear, thanks for listening. Talk to you later."

I want to think Mrs. Hicks loves language arts and wants the kids to learn. I even got my trusted senior, Sarah, aside to find out what her classes are really like. She told me one time when Mrs. Hicks fell asleep, the kids put chewed gum on the soles of her shoes. "Another time she fell on the floor forgetting to grab the arms of her roller chair," she said.

"But I'm sure she gives her classes cool writing prompts," I said hopefully.

"No, she gives us workbook pages to do or takes us to the computers in the library and disappears. Mrs. Yazzie has to watch us."

I don't know if Mr. Howard will keep her next year, but I would hate to see her go. To me, she's harmless, a big 55-year-old baby. I can enjoy her escapades without having to teach or discipline. She brings much amusement to my otherwise dull or frustrating days in my own classroom, and like a grandchild, I can always send her away.

DAY 98
Too Much Information

In order to encourage communication between the school district and the families it serves and to enhance the school climate, Madison sent home a survey for parents and students. Responses to the question, *What would improve the school?* are as follows:

- they should have better lunch and fair disciplin and cleaner bathrooms and they need to take the troublemakers out of the school like anger problem people out
- I am not shor
- I think the discipline system of the school needs to be more serious and not warning after warning.
- better ways to teach us education
- what would improve the school is better teachers and expecially Spanish, because we tend to really not learn anything and I really don't understand the class and we need it for college
- if our school had teachers that werent straight out of school themselves I think we would do much better
- new teachers
- wider variety of classes
- Better lunches, more outings, or more reconizion to honors students.
- More elective classes and a better foreign language teacher.
- I suppose more time for math, more disapine because sometimes the teachers let the students keep going on and on and it is really distracting as well as the bullying issue.

•A new one.

•your mom

•Better foreign language. I've been in there for almost a whole semester and I can't hold a full conversation yet.

•1. NEW PRINCIPLE 2. New Gym Teacher. 3. Better subs that let you interact with your peers instead of acting like this is Alcatraz Prison. 4. More freedoms in the school. 5. More ability for self expression.

•enething and everything.

•New principal

•School lunch! It is old and gross. I don't feel like the first lady would be impressed.

•peepee

•reading whiting and speak

•to get rid of all the corrupt teachers, to get rid of uniforms (this is america. not the soviet union) we should be able to express ourselves. to get a new principal, and new food. the lunch here tastes disgusting. I wouldn't even feed my dog our school's lunch.

•Better teachers, NEW PRINCIPAL, better staff overall, and if we are suppose to have uniforms then it should be enforced. My opinion is that ever since our new principal the school is going down hill day by day.

•The Spanish teacher. she is cool but we are not learning that much spanish.

•I want MADDISIN TOO HAVE a CHOKLET WETER FOOTEN.

•A better Spanish teacher that actually teaches you something.

•New lunch… sometimes we'll have cheeseburgers then the next day we'll have chicken nuggets or the same cheeseburgers as the day before!

•the teachers are excuse my "french" ass-holes, they are rude and show biased opinions/favoritism!

•Mathematics could be more challenging. I have already learned everything we are learning at my grade level last year. The lunches could be better the chicken and hamburgers are not always done they are pink, bullying should be watched at a higher level

•The school lunches, sometimes the chicken and hambureger is pink or not fully cooked.

•No assigned seats

•Idk

•HELPP!!

•BETTER TEACHERS AND BETTER PRINCIBLES!!!!!!!!!!!!!!!!!!!!!!

•Get rid of these roaches because it is really nasty. This school need to get feildtrips like when we are learning about something good maybe we would really like to pay more attention in it won't be so boring.

•Better education, more exterminators for the bugs also more better tasting lunch (that is cooked all the way)

•I would make it to were all the classes teach us something.

•makeing the class more adiqueit.

•If there were tudiring, some classes that tought different languages (I vote for japanese or chinese). Something you would get at the end of the year to drive students to want to succed.

•getting a new spanish teacher.

•if they'd stop worrying so much about the little things such as dress code etc

•more oppertunities

•I wish that we can yoos a phone.

•Better lunches, shorter school days, less school days, no homework, no school work. You could take care of all these things by not having school.

The following comments came from the same survey.

•Nothing, I like this school.

•just to work hard

•If I was in charge I will tell everybody to pay atenshion.

•Manners

•More time of school work

•Keep it as it is

•Working a lot harder

•Nothing, I do well in all subjects.

•To not always play around. Get my science and social studies grades up. Just doing the right thing.

•Respect, a lot of kids will just ignore their assignments or certain teachers.

•In my opinion I think the school is fine just the way it is, nothing needs to improve to me.

•harder classes for some students

•If the students were more respectful. I feel like some of my school work is too easy for me and that I should be challenging myself a little more.

•My high expectations

•Well I don't really know. I think my school is the best it could be. I love it.

•If I do good in every subject and be nice to people probably.

After reading these two lists, a pop quiz is in order:

Which list did the administration like best?

Students on which list have a better chance of success?

Which list was greatly entertaining?

What foreign language needs a lift?

What is wrong in the cafeteria?

Who is not popular?

How can all these problems be solved?

If you score a 100%, you're hired to come in and turn this into a Blue Ribbon School.

DAY 99
A Call to Consciousness

Today I lost it during senior government. "This is my worst class of the day. You're loud, obnoxious, immature, disrespectful, and disinterested in academics. I cannot complete one sentence without being interrupted. My other classes are fine. You are seniors. This should be my best class, but every day I dread fourth bell."

Surprisingly, my tirade shut them up and I continued listing ways candidates fund their campaigns. "What's that poster for?" asked Oumar.

"That's for U.S. history," I snapped. "You know, for my freshmen who are ten times more focused than you seniors."

"Mrs. Ball," he replied, "just answer the question. You don't have to go back over all that."

Oumar was right. I should have just answered his question. There was no problem at that moment. I was still shell shocked from his previous disruption and assumed it would continue. I was unconscious—not seeing, thinking, or acting in the present.

At least I didn't dig myself into a hole. "Sorry, Oumar, that's a poster of Iwo Jima, a major battle of WWII. That's the second time you taught me something."

His face lit up. "Yeah, remember when you kept saying *Islum.* It's *Islam.* I know. I'm a Muslim."

"Yes, thanks to you I pronounce it correctly now." The first step to teaching, I thought, is willingness to learn from even the most challenging of students.

But Oumar wasn't going to exactly have his way with me. I walked to his desk and tapped his book. "Now put your religious ideals into practice and finish this section."

DAY 100
Walt

Today I fled from my classroom without my coat when I heard the garbage can rolling down the hall at 3:15. Although it was 20 degrees out, I preferred freezing on the way home than getting trapped by Walt, the custodian for the second floor. One afternoon I passed him on my way out and he stopped me to talk. He remarked how destructive the kids are to school property and described the messes he has to clean up. "The kids smear soap all over the mirrors and pour it on the floors. Then they stuff paper towels in the sink drains and turn on the water. They pee on the walls and clog up the toilets with great wads of toilet paper. I wonder if they treat their own homes the same way."

"I wish they would put half that imagination and effort into their work," I said. "I know what you mean. I buy Kleenex for the room with my own money and they use it, throw it on the floor, and refuse to pick it up." I didn't mind talking to Walt the first time I met him. I was comforted to learn that the kids were bad in other areas of the school and not just in my room. I considered him an ally.

The next afternoon he stopped me and talked about the work he was doing around his house. I got all the details about his new front door and his screened in porch. I was getting impatient. I didn't give a damn about what he was saying, and I didn't have twenty minutes to waste after school. I listened politely and finally excused myself. "I have to go to the hospital and visit my dad."

"Oh, what hospital is he in? I was in rehab in Mercy Mount Airy after my bypass surgery. Is he on the third floor? That's where I was, a very nice big room for all the exercises they give you."

"Goodbye," I said having no choice but to cut him off and walk away.

A few days later, I was sitting at my desk after school trying to finish plans for the next day. He came into my room with the vacuum sweeper, but instead of working he parked himself at a desk in front of mine and began talking. I told myself to be attentive for five minutes, and surely he'd get back on the job. He gave a dissertation about how competent and respected he was at his former job. Then he went on about his wife's dental work, and his grandchild's birthday party. After twenty minutes, I realized he was there for the duration and that no amount of time being polite would satisfy him. "Did you ever eat at that Red Squirrel on Galbraith Road? My wife and I like the sauerkraut and mett special on Tuesdays."

I packed my papers and got up. "Have a good evening," I said.

"Oh, how is your dad? I bet you're going to the hospital." He was totally unwilling to end the conversation. I wanted to cry. I had just lost a half hour and my work was not done. He was holding me hostage, and the only way to escape was to be downright rude.

"He's getting better. Goodbye." All the way to my car I fumed. It was 3:45. I had been in that building since 7:30. Was I supposed to baby sit the custodian for another two hours? Wasn't he supposed to be working? When I meet the other custodians, we have a pleasant exchange and then go about our own business.

One afternoon I was working on my computer in the back of the room and Walt came in to empty the trash. "Oh, you're letting your hair grow," he said. I turned off the computer.

"I'm not letting it grow, I just don't have time for it." I left the room, careful not to make eye contact or engage with him further.

Since that day it has been a race to get out of the building before he gets to my room. Sometimes I hide in the attendance office if I still have work to do. I often ask myself what kind of a human being I am to consciously snub another human being. Am I so busy that I can't stop to talk to a lonely old man? Although I feel badly for him and am embarrassed by the way I act, let's face it, I can't be all things to all people. If I hadn't fled without my coat this afternoon, I'd still be stuck at school this very minute enduring Walt.

DAY 101
Patriarchs

Study hall is the worst bell of the day. It's right after lunch and the kids are all wound up from the frenzy of the cafeteria. Plus, kids refuse to study during study hall. They consider it their time to hang out. I've tried everything, seating charts, a list of rules, and office referrals, but I can't control the kids. I'd rather teach another class than police kids and watch them waste time. Fridays are the worst. They are steadfastly in the "school is out" mindset. I don't know why I eat lunch. Study hall churns my stomach.

Today Justin Barnes, the school's wannabe thug, came in, wandered around the students' desks as though he were at a party, and started to socialize. I, of course, am a nobody, invisible to him and his personal agenda. He had his back to me and ignored me when I told him to sit down and get out something to do. I rejoiced when a pack of cigarettes dropped on the floor. This is a clear infraction of the school rules, and now I had a good reason to send him out. "Justin, you can't have cigarettes. Go to the office."

"They just dropped out of my pocket," he snapped at me.

"I don't care what they did, you can't bring cigarettes to school."

"Oh stop talking, shut up. Where's your husband?"

"Go to the office." In shock and trying to keep my lunch down I wrote up his referral.

"You ought to try it sometime," he lashed at me as he left the room. The others laughed.

I'm fairly easy going after 25 years in a public school. I don't get all uptight when the F-word flies inadvertently, and I ignore random off color comments. I've had spitballs blown at me and pencil points just missing my eyes. But a direct personal attack on me or another, especially with sexual connotations, is outrageous. According to him, I have no right to enforce the school rules and demand order in my classroom. Since I'm a woman I need to be silenced, and moreover, by a man and sex.

I was floored by this kid's male chauvinism and his cruel tone of voice. My father was all for women as he raised four daughters, and my husband has always treated me with respect. I'm no women's libber or feminist and I don't get easily offended. This kid crossed the line.

I don't need to get fucked, I wanted to tell him, *I need you to follow the rules.* I wanted to ask him, who asked me where my husband was, *Where's your wife-beater undershirt?* But I am silenced, kept in my place. My only recourse was a flimsy referral upon which I wrote, *cigarettes and sexual harassment.* No type of writing could have conveyed to Mr. Howard, the principal, my humiliation and outrage. No skill on my part could have made him care.

I took the cigarettes to the office and lay them on Mr. Howard's desk. "We'll talk about it," he told Justin looking past me. *Talk about what? I wanted to scream. You made these rules. Shouldn't I enforce them? What are you talking to a 17-year-old about?*

Fifteen minutes later Justin was back in my room and continued to socialize and disrupt the order I had gained while he was gone. At the end of the day when I checked my mailbox, there was no response to my referral and no consequence for Justin.

I wanted to raise a fuss. I wanted to tell Mr. Howard that sexual harassment is a serious matter and that I don't want any further contact with Justin. I want him out of my study hall. But instead I was a good girl and a good sport and chose not to cause any problems.

DAY 102
Air Pollution

It's a challenge to get the kids in their seats and settled for fourth bell, the bell right after lunch. I left the teachers' lounge early to get the books and folders on the students' desks so when they came in at 12:15 they'd know I meant business. At 12:20 all the kids were in their assigned seats with books open and their guided reading packet at hand to jot down notes and answers. I pulled a name from my "you'd better know the place" box and called on Frankie to read the next passage from *Hiroshima*. Frankie knew the place, the kids were quiet and engaged, and I was as smug as I could be. If anyone were to walk past my room and glance in, I'd receive the teacher of the year award. I love it when an administrator, a fellow teacher, or a parent comes to my room at such a time.

"They were coming down with radiation sickness," read Frankie. I looked up to see that Robin, on Frankie's right, had left her assigned seat and went back to a desk by the window. Patrick, on his left, scooted his desk toward the front of the room and messed up my neat row.

"Robin, what are you doing? Patrick, get your desk back in line."

"You don't smell that, Ms. Ball?" said Patrick. "Frankie farted and I'm not sitting next to him."

"Where are your social skills?" I said. "If you were being interviewed for a job you really wanted, and someone passed gas, is that how you'd act? Frankie, keep on reading, the rest of you grow up."

"Nausea, diarrhea, hair loss, and a general feeling of malaise were effects of this mysterious bomb."

More commotion made me look up again. Four more students had left their seats to get away from Frankie. "God, Frankie, put a plug in your butt," yelled Steven.

I pulled another name from the box. Kendra began reading and I didn't fight the seating arrangement, satisfied that most kids were still following the book. "There was a rumor going around that a single plane had sprayed a poison over the whole city causing the electrical wires to ignite. No one could enter Hiroshima..."

"Frankie, what did you eat for lunch?" cried James. By this time, Frankie had no one within yards of him, but he just sat there grinning. The kids were at the windowsill with their heads hanging out or at the door with their heads in the hallway. Just then the principal walked by, looked into the room, rolled his eyes, and kept on walking. In a matter of minutes my chances for the teacher of the year were ruined by something unseen and unheard.

The smell was so bad even I had to abandon my social skills. I sprayed air freshener around the room and turned on the fan. "Frankie, tomorrow if you have to pass gas, you have my permission ahead of time to leave the room."

DAY 103
To a Different Tune

Bethany has an IEP, Individual Education Program. That is, she's a slow learner. She's normal looking, but a little off as a student. She's not disrespectful, but refuses to read when it's her turn and refuses to answer questions even when something is written on her paper. I have stopped trying to encourage or force her to participate. She's perfectly happy being skipped over. "I just don't like to talk in front of people," she explains. When she does raise her hand, it looks as though she's getting ready to say the most profound thing ever. She pauses for a minute, then asks to use the restroom.

Today I tried working with her alone, thinking I could get her better engaged and give her a better understanding of our current topic. "Bethany, get your questions out and open your book to the chapter on the Industrial Revolution." I sat beside her and was ready to dig in. "Number 1, what characteristics of Great Britain enabled it to lead the Industrial Revolution? Look in the first column, third paragraph."

"Do you want to see my drawings?" She pulled out two sketches of cats from her folder.

"Those are good, Bethany. You're a good artist."

"Here, you can have one."

I didn't want the cat. I wanted her to understand the Industrial Revolution. I hate just giving IEP students a C or D without trying to teach them something. Besides, these kids have to pass the state test too. I got a push pin and tacked the cat on my bulletin board. I sat back down and pointed in her text. "What is the climate like in Great Britain?"

"It says warm and moist."

"Right, what else does it say?"

"Ms. Ball, I wrote a poem last night, want to read it?"

"Let's answer these questions first since I have time right now to work with you. How did a warm and moist climate help the Industrial Revolution? What is Britain's main agricultural product?"

She searched the paragraph. "Cotton."

"Exactly, a warm and moist climate is ideal for growing cotton. So Great Britain led the world in cotton production and textile manufacturing. Do you know what textiles are?"

"I guess cloth."

"Good, kids your age worked all day in dusty dirty factories making cloth instead of going to school." I thought talking about kids might pull her in. "What other characteristics can you find?"

"Ms. Ball, guess what?"

"Here, Bethany, what does it say about Britain's government? Remember we learned the difference between a market economy and a command economy? Britain encouraged private business growth instead of directing production from the government like other European countries."

"I'm making sugar cookies tonight. I'll bring you some tomorrow."

"Yum, I love your sugar cookies. Let's find one more characteristic before the bell rings. It has to do with Britain's geography."

"But don't you want me to read you my poem?"

I gave up. The politicians and education experts who require these kids to pass the state test can sit down here and tutor Bethany themselves. "Sure, Bethany, take it away. But promise me you'll work on these questions for homework."

At bell's end Bethany and I had finished two questions with questionable understanding. I had counted on getting through all ten.

Tomorrow, she won't have her homework, but I guarantee she'll have sugar cookies, another sketch, and a homemade sympathy card for the secretary who just lost her father.

DAY 104
TESA

Screw it. I'm going to take a tranquilizer. I'm not going to try and sleep without it when I know I'll be up churning all night. I've been around public school teens for over twenty years and they still upset me. I guess I didn't call upon my TESA strategies today. TESA stands for Teacher Expectations/ Student Achievement, another miracle program that enlightened me and my coworkers during our after school in-service. So what was I expected to do with my nightmarish seniors in fourth bell to promote their achievement?

TESA is a touchy feely educational philosophy. The teacher elicits high academic performance in a nurturing environment, instills student self-esteem and well-being, and provides engaging lesson plans. For example, one master teacher's secret to a high performing classroom with no discipline problems is a big dispenser of lotion. Some students have dry ashy skin and the lotion shows the kids she cares about their personal needs. TESA should stand for Teachers Enabling Students Always. But like a good TESA teacher, I bought a 24 ounce Lubriderm and placed it on the window sill. By the second day it had disappeared. As for lessons, I thought I had an engaging one when I brought in news articles and taped them all around the classroom. I gave the kids a sheet of questions and put them on a scavenger hunt for the answers. We're supposed to get them out of their seats, moving around, and involved in their learning. By the end of class, there were more moustaches on Obama, horns on John Boehner, and fangs on Hillary Clinton than answers to the questions.

Today a fight almost broke out in my room. I told Ron to tuck his shirt in as he entered my senior government class. Ron is a National Honor Society member and valedictorian of the class. He is supposed to be a role model, yet every day I have to tell him to tuck his shirt in. He thinks he's a genius because he got a 27 on his ACT. Anyway, he tucked it in, sat down, and started texting under his desk which is also against the school rules. Like it wasn't obvious what he was doing. I chose to ignore it though, not having the energy to confront him and risk a tantrum. We're supposed to teach, deal with behavior, and enforce the school rules all at once.

I began class by asking for volunteers to put the homework on the board. I bought colored dry erase markers to liven things up. Kenny got up with his notebook and started writing. The back of his shirt had come out but the front was tucked in.

"You ain't tell Kenny to tuck his shirt in," Ron said to me.

"Shut up," Kenny said to Ron.

"No, it ain't fair. I gotta tuck mine in and you don't," whined the genius.

"You wanna fight about it?" challenged Kenny.

"Yeah, I'll fight about it," said Ron.

I did nothing at first because I thought they were just kidding. These are common occurrences and I was waiting for this one to pass. In TESA language I was trying to *defuse* the situation. But I saw they weren't kidding, shocked that two 18-year-olds would pick a fight about an untucked shirt. Kenny stepped towards Ron and put his fists up.

"Stop it," I yelled.

Kenny noticed me and went to the doorway. He put his fists up again and said, "Come on, I'll fight you in the hall."

Ron just sat there and taunted the thug. He was too much of a wimp to go out and fight him. Kenny was pumping his fists and moving his feet like Muhammad Ali, and Ron kept egging him on. Afraid Kenny would come back in the room after him, I pressed the call button. "There's about to be a fight in my room," I said. The resource officer took Kenny away and the principal came for Ron a few minutes later.

So then I was supposed to teach something. The rest of the kids were laughing and discussing the whole scene, shouting back and forth to each other. "Shut up," I yelled, "Just shut up. The next person I hear, I'll press the

call button for you too." Miraculously no one challenged me. I carried out
a semblance of a lesson plan for the rest of the bell shaking all the while. I
wondered what practices our TESA expert would have recommended to avoid
this disaster. I'd love to see him teach this class. I guess I didn't have lotion for
Kenny or a stimulating enough lesson for Ron. After 25 years in education,
I'm still waiting for policies including student as well as teacher expectations.

DAY 105
Old Fogeys

I used to disdain old fogeys. My grandpa, for instance, always said, "Doesn't anybody cook anymore?" Customers flooded into his shoe store with McDonald's just when he wanted to go home for lunch. My grandma's cooking was something to go home for. My dad, always impeccably dressed in business attire, criticized the general public dress code of jeans, gym shoes, tee shirts, and baseball caps worn indoors. "Doesn't anyone know how to dress up? Look how sloppy people look now days." Mr. Schlotman, an elderly gentleman from our country club, could not tolerate rock music. "Doesn't anyone listen to big band anymore? That's real music. Rock and Roll is trash." I flinched with annoyance at the old fogeys' comments. I love to eat out, dress down and listen up to hard rock.

Now I'm looked upon as an old fogey teacher because I complain about computers and cell phones. Doesn't anyone go to the library anymore? When I assign a research paper, the students go straight online for an instant solution to what should be a two week process. When I was in school, we went to the library, checked out books, took notes on index cards, made an outline, hand wrote a rough draft in our own words, and then typed a final copy. Computers are great for research and efficient clean typing, but they can't think, and students' work shows it. For a typical report, kids type in their topic and the information instantly appears before them. They highlight sentences here, paragraphs there, paste them onto a word document, add in a few pictures, and the report is done. Plagiarized sentences abound. *It is estimated that Canada contributed to 10% of the D-Day force. The invasion was preceded by a massive aerial bombardment of German communications. Elizabeth Stanton gave birth to seven children.* "Kids, no one says 'give birth to.' I read your writing every day. Don't you know I know that you don't write like that?"

The report has to get done though because the kids have to hurry and check their cell phones. Most students have them, even in the elementary grades. Although they violate school policy, kids make calls in the rest rooms, halls, and walking to and from school. If I catch them using their cell phones they look at me as if to say, "See, don't I look important?" I want to yell at them. "No, you don't look important. Doctors and policemen look important with cell phones. No one needs to get in touch with you and you don't need to reach anyone. If you want to do something impressive, turn in your assignments."

I'm sure kids and many adults think I'm an old fogey. Pants drooping below the butt and multiple piercings don't even bother me as much as kids constantly hanging on computers and cell phones. Students need to go to the library, then to a paper and pencil copy, then to the computer. They need to earn a degree, get a job, and then they will have a reason to own a cell phone.

DAY 106
Mrs. Hicks

Mrs. Hicks returned to school after an eight day absence. She said she had pneumonia, her husband broke his hip, and her cousin died. She wasn't pale, didn't look sad, and was as plump as ever. She surely didn't use any of her time off at the hair stylist.

"I feel so weak," she told me at the copy machine in the office." She looked plenty strong to me but I humored her anyway.

"It's good to see you back," I said.

"Howard said I'm gone after this year. Look at the evaluation he wrote me from the observation before I got sick."

It wasn't my problem, but I looked at it to be polite. She got *satisfactory* in a few categories but *basic* and *unsatisfactory* in most.

"When I walk by your room, it seems you're doing a great job with the kids," I said.

"I asked Howard to evaluate me again to see if I took his suggestions for improvement. I have a great lesson in mind. You know, Dear, I'm looking for a new job. There's this little elementary school close to my house. The pay is less, but it's a trade off for all this stress around here." She took a paper from the copier. "See, I have a doctor's excuse."

The homeroom bell rang and we went to our rooms. At lunch she ate two thick meatloaf sandwiches. *There's nothing weak about her appetite*, I thought. Mrs. Hicks might not be back next year, so I'd better enjoy her antics now.

DAY 107
Casualties

The bell had just rung. It was time to face third period. I stood in front of my U.S. studies class and looked around the room. Of twenty-two students, only fourteen were present. I sighed, then walked up and down the rows to check off last night's homework. Three senior boys had their heads down. They looked like they had hangovers—passed out, strung out. I stepped by them gingerly, afraid one would vomit if I happened to bump a desk. Two students were copying another one's work right in front of me. "None of you get credit," I said and started to move on.

"That ain't fair," Colleen snapped at me. "I did *my* work."

"Then don't give it away," I said. "The others aren't learning anything copying off of you."

"That's bull," said Colleen, and the other two agreed.

I tensed up but continued checking for completed assignments. I stopped at Rhonetta's desk. She was drawing cartoons. I did not take them from her, having learned the hard way not to cross into anyone's personal space. "Rhonetta," I said, "could you put your pictures away and get out your WWI questions?" She ignored me and continued to draw. I could imagine her thinking, *This class ain't important and you're a lousy teacher.*

I started to believe this myself as I reassessed the situation. Of the fourteen present I'd lost three to hangovers, three to pouting, and one to cartoons. Of the seven left, only three students had the assignment complete. That wasn't exactly what I'd had in mind when I made up the questions the other day with so much enthusiasm. *What a class*, I thought.

The remaining four students had their heads up at least and their papers out to follow along. I conducted class with seven students. My three real students, Christina, Brittany and Justin got lots of turns to answer. I felt badly for them. They deserved to be in a more dynamic atmosphere. Getting through this bell was like plodding through a battlefield with three allies, four nonaligned, four enemies, and the rest dead. I went through the motions. I tried to fake it for the seven, despite my disappointment that I hadn't even reached one third of the class.

"The soldiers were starving in the trenches. The U.S. citizens planted Victory Gardens to conserve food so it could be sent to Europe." My voice was weak and hesitant. I was trying to make my students believe in the importance of history when just then I couldn't believe in it myself. I was a failure, a flop, a fraud. *What can I do to rev these kids up?* I asked myself.

"I gotta use the restroom," Bernice called out.

"You know the rules. Bring me your planner and I'll sign you out."

"I don't have it," she said.

"Then you can't leave the room." I tried to act businesslike, but I was starting to shake. "The side that can feed the troops will win. 'Food will win the war,' said Herbert Hoover." I felt about as popular as that president during the Great Depression.

"I gotta use it," shouted Bernice. She stood up and got right in my face. The class looked at me. If I let her go without her planner, I thought, others will want to, and my system will break down. My rules will have no credibility. If I don't let her go I'm a cold-hearted bitch. Maybe she really needs to go. Maybe I should bend my rules and be more compassionate. Then I'll be taken for a pushover and everyone will take advantage of me and my class will turn into chaos. Everyone was waiting. I had to think fast.

"Bernice, if you have to go that badly, I'll write you a pass, but not for free. You owe me a fifteen-minute detention after school." If she's sincere, I thought, she'll take the DT. If she's faking, she'll sit down. Everyone looked at her instead of me.

"Never mind," she said. The class seemed satisfied. I'd given her an out, but didn't abandon my rules. I started to breathe again.

The bell rang and the kids moved on to fourth period. One student shook the three sleepers and they lumbered out. As badly as class had gone, I still owned it, and the floor was vomit free at that. There had been lots of casualties, but I wasn't one of them. Not much to brag about, I thought, as I returned to my desk to brace myself for the next battle.

DAY 108
March Madness

New school supplies in September, students resolute
History facts, science, math they compute.
By March missed assignments, notes to a buddy
This is boring, I hate school. Who wants to study?

DAY 109
Waiting It Out

I'm an imposter. The kids deserve better. Or do I deserve better? What a play school. I'm making it through the year but it doesn't feel right. I don't know how much longer I can do this. It seems that teaching should get better each year, but it's getting worse by the second—bigger class sizes, more classes to teach, more state requirements to meet, and the kids, my God, the kids.

Today there was a fight in the hall outside my classroom after lunch. To my utter dismay they were *my* students coming to *my* class. *Shit*, I thought. *I don't want to deal with this again today.* No such luck. Short stocky Kendra stormed into the room after loose-jointed 6'4" Dion. She looked like a rhinoceros chasing a giraffe. "I don't know who you think you is, saying stuff 'bout me behind my back. If you want to say somethin,' say it to my face."

"Ain't nobody sayin' nothin' to you," said Dion.

Kendra stood up on a chair to get level with him. "That's the point, you sayin' stuff '*bout* me, not *to* me."

"Who wanna be in your shit anyway," said Dion.

"Fuck you," said Kendra and she shoved him. Luckily he didn't shove back. I didn't know if his gentlemanly instincts prevailed or if he was afraid of her. I know I am.

"Fuck you," he said and sat down. Kendra was still standing on the chair towering over him.

I walked over and put my finger on the call button. "Hey, knock it off or I'm calling Officer Sands." Kendra went to her seat and I tried to start class over the tumult. "Hello out there, remember me? This is senior government."

God help this country, I thought, *if this is what high schools are sending to the workforce.* "Get out your homework and I'll come around to check it."

I put three columns on the board, one for state legislatures, one for the federal legislature, and one for similarities. I handed the name box to Amber. She called on students to go up and fill in information. Thank God for Sarah, Cody and Amber. I relaxed a little until Tommie started drumming on the desk and rapping. I approached him with my clipboard. "Tommie, please stop. Do you have your homework?"

"Naw," he said with his baby face grin, and continued to drum.

"Tommie don't get no Cheez-its," sang a few boys. I'd been giving him snacks from my lunch to bribe him into compliance.

"Amber, call three more names," I said.

Tracy was walking around in the back of the room and mumbling to himself. No way can I get him to sit in his assigned seat. I've kicked him out of class and written him up many times; but the principal keeps sending him back and Tracy keeps doing whatever he wants to do. "Tracy, please be quiet," I said.

"Oh my bad, Ms. Ball." He started talking about the NCAA pairings to a few others in the back. Today an XXL grimy white polo hung on his medium frame. The uniform policy requires kids to tuck in their shirts, but no matter how many times I remind Tracy, it's always out. He's a nice kid when you talk to him privately. After school one day he told me he lives on his own with his little brother. His mom kicked him out of the house because he kept getting sent to juvenile detention for drugs. He wants to graduate, but he has to work to pay his rent so he doesn't have time for his homework.

"Tracy, be quiet."

"But see, Ms. Ball, I don't never get to talk to my buddies after school cause I'm always working. So that's why I talk in class."

"I'm sorry," I said, "but this is not your opportunity to socialize."

"My bad, I'll stop." Less than a minute later he was back at it talking March Madness with Dalton and Dakota. Meanwhile, Tommie was at the pencil sharpener gyrating to an imaginary song.

"Ms. Ball, don't look so stressed," said Amber who was still running the lesson up at the board. Hannah, always prepared, went up and added a new fact.

"Yeah, it's Friday," said Dion. "Can't we talk for the rest of the bell?"

"If I did that, I wouldn't feel right about myself. I owe you fifty minutes of instruction whether you want it or not." This was about more than being conscientious. I knew that even ten minutes of idle time could invite another fight.

"But we'll feel right about it," said Dion.

Everyone laughed, but I plodded through the lesson. I checked over the information and the students read what they wrote. They had to talk over Tracy, Tommie, Dakota and Dalton who were still at it in the back.

I wanted so much better for my students. *What classroom management strategy can I employ now? Will Power*, I thought. I passed out *Fahrenheit 451*, our enrichment novel. I turned on the tape player and tried to lull them into submission. For the remaining time the kids settled in to the author's voice.

DAY 110
The Bottom of It

Donovan stinks. No one in fifth bell wants to sit next to him. I seat him in the back by the windows and have to keep one open even in the dead of winter. I try and seat hearty, good-natured boys around him. Whoever is unfortunate enough to get stuck next to him pulls his shirt up to his face to cover his nose, a behavior I would normally reprimand. When the class is over I quickly clean his seat with Clorox wipes and open every window to air out the room for the next class. No matter what I do the kids come in saying, "It stinks in here." I want to scream, *I know it does, I've been living in it for the past hour!* Donovan costs me at least 15 minutes of academic learning time each day. The other teachers complain about him too, but no one is willing to take action.

A few weeks ago I was determined to get to the bottom of it. I talked to the principal who brushed me off saying that Donovan has a medical problem. *Bullshit,* I thought. I went to our school nurse who looked up his file and found no such thing.

"I'll call his parents," she assured me.

Finally, I thought, *we're getting somewhere.* The next morning his homeroom teacher reported that he smelled like baby powder. By the time he reached my class in the late afternoon, the French bath had worn off and the same old dirty butt smell permeated my room. I went back to the nurse and delivered a tirade. "There is no reason that in the 21st century in the United States of America that any student should stink. What does he need? I'll buy him soap, shampoo, deodorant, laundry detergent and several new changes of clothes. A burly 9th grade boy should be able to take care of himself. If he does have loose bowels as his dad claims, a system needs to be put into place. He should come to the bathroom in your office, wipe off with Wet Ones, change his clothes, and return to class. This isn't that hard."

"When I talk to him he won't say anything," said the nurse.

"Well, somebody has to say something," I said. "It's oppressive and unhealthy in my room and it's unfair to the other students."

Still, no one acts, not Donovan, not his parents, not the nurse, not the principal. This is their responsibility. Why am I the only one who is not in denial? I'm his history teacher. It is not my place to address his hygiene or so called "loose bowels." No one plans my lessons for me or grades my papers.

Today was no different. Donovan came to my 5th bell class and stunk up the room. When he left I had to hurry and make it tolerable for 6th bell. I have not gotten to the bottom of it except to say that his bottom stinks.

I've since learned why Donovan's clothes and body don't get washed. His mother is an invalid unable to provide practical everyday hygiene for others. I have stopped fighting the smell in my classroom. I can't apply my Western mindset to fix this problem. It's out of my control. I simply continue to wipe his desk, spray the room, and open the windows.

DAY 111
Permission

Robby is new this year and I don't know him that well. I've gathered that
he's an average student with a temper and I'm never quite sure what he will
do next. "Can I use the restroom?" he asked me several days ago near the end
of class.

"No," I said, "the bell's going to ring in a few minutes. You can go
between classes."

"I'm going now," he said, packing up his books and leaving sans permission.

The next day he asked me if he could go to his locker because he forgot
his book.

"No, Robby," I insisted. "You're supposed to come to class prepared. Mr.
Howard doesn't want anyone in the halls during class. Sit down and look off
with Ryan."

"I ain't doin' that," he said disappearing from the room.

He was gone a lot longer than it would have taken to go to his locker, and
he returned empty handed. I decided to ignore it since no one else demanded
to leave, and Ryan didn't mind sharing his book when Robby finally sat down.

Today, ten minutes into class, Robby interrupted me while going over the
homework. "Ms. Ball, can I go to Mrs. Barton's room? I left my homework
down there. Exasperated, I ignored his request. "Can I?" he persisted.

"Robby, what are you asking me for? You'll do whatever you want anyway."

He sat down, pulled his homework from his book bag and raised his hand
for the next question. *Talk about reverse psychology,* I thought. *Who knows what
strategy will work next?*

DAY 112
Mandela's Mindset

Because of his recent death, I focused my government current events lesson on Nelson Mandela. We talked about his family life, his 27 years in prison, and his rise as the first black president of South Africa. "What U.S. president vetoed the anti-apartheid act?" I asked. Breanna's face lit up as she raised her hand. I called on her.

"What's my grade in here?" she said.

In an instant, my demeanor changed from enthusiasm to anger. "It would be a lot better than it is if you'd ask better questions," I snapped.

Mickey broke the ice. "Ronald Reagan."

"But Congress overrode it," added Matthew.

"Perfect. Those are the types of responses I'm looking for," I said glaring at Breanna. "Now, what was Mandela's brilliant political tactic?" I continued.

Drew raised his hand. "Reconciliation with his enemies, then actually including them in his government."

"Thanks, Drew, I'm impressed how thoroughly you read the article. "Last question, what award did Mandela receive?" Breanna was the only one to raise her hand but I resented calling on her. For effect, I paused before saying, "In honor of Mandela and reconciliation, I'll give you another try."

"The Nobel Peace Prize," she said. "He didn't receive it alone. He shared it with F.W. De Klerk, South Africa's last white president."

I smiled and the class applauded. "May your grade continue to speak for itself."

DAY 113
IEP Refused

Antwan Adonis has an IEP. That stands for Individual Education Program. It really stands for an excuse to do very little work and act however you want. Antwan comes late to first bell most days. He strolls in with headphones, sunglasses, iPhone, and hat, all things students aren't allowed. Just when I have the class settled and engaged, Antwan walks from buddy to buddy giving high fives, fist bumps, and brother handshakes. He talks about basketball, girlfriends and the latest gossip, oblivious that I'm in the room teaching government, a course all seniors need to graduate. It does little good to send him to the office. I've done that over a dozen times already, complaining that dealing with one student wastes ten minutes of my lesson every day. IEP kids can't get disciplined like regular ed. students according to state law. The letters might as well stand for *I'm Enabling Perfectly*.

Today Antwan was fashionably late making his entrance in a black suit and vest, a purple dress shirt and tie, and shiny black shoes. I had to admit he did look like Adonis, but I was in no mood to compliment him. "What's the occasion?" I asked.

"I just felt like it," he replied, pleased that I noticed his attire.

You mean you felt like posturing in front of the class, school work the farthest thing from your agenda, I wanted to retort. "Antwan, where is your government book? We're reading the introduction to chapter 8."

"My stuff's in Miss Baxter's room," he replied. Why did I ask? Miss Baxter is the special ed. teacher who supports the IEP students. Whenever they don't have their homework or materials, they're "in Miss Baxter's room." That room, that reference is their *get out of jail free ticket,* as though all responsibility lies in that room and none with themselves.

"Sit down then and look with Shaq." I finally remembered the rest of the class, angry that again I let one student steal so much time. "Let's get back to our introduction. Donnie, it's your turn for the next paragraph. Antwan, please stop talking."

"I have Turrets," he said.

"I'm not qualified to deal with Turrets, so knock it off or you'll go to the office. See if anyone there will play your games."

That insult worked for a few minutes, but I finally had to kick him out. Antwan wouldn't stay in his seat or stop talking.

Later, he came back to get his assignment *to do in Miss Baxter's room.* "Are we cool?" He flashed a big beautiful smile and held out his hand for a brother shake which I refused. Instead, I shoved two worksheets in his hand.

"We'll be cool if ever I get any work or compliance from you. Until then, get out of here. This isn't all about you. I have plenty of other students to help who come to school every day and manage to stay in the room the whole bell."

DAY 114
Paradox

It was 7:45 and I was rushing to write notes on the board for my first bell government class. Although the students already had the notes on the guide I passed out yesterday, I found it necessary to spell everything out in front of them in colored markers especially for the *visual learners*.

Devonte arrived before his buddies and acknowledged me. "Ms. Ball, I'm going to work real hard for you today."

"For me? I already have my high school diploma."

"Oh, I know. It's for me."

"Did you do your homework?"

"Oh snap. I left my books in Miss Baxter's room yesterday."

"Then how can you work hard for anyone? Hurry and get them before the bell rings."

Devonte came back empty handed and sunk into his seat. I began class passing out copies of the Gettysburg Address as well as a background article. It was November 19th, its 150th anniversary. I wanted to honor that special date before continuing our regular work. To get the kids engaged, I called on each to read a few lines.

Halfway through the article, it was Devonte's turn. "Where we at?" he asked looking around for help. Shaq kindly pointed to the place, and Devonte read as though he were Lincoln himself even pronouncing *peroration* without a flaw.

When the students had finished I asked the obvious question. "During what war was this speech given?"

"The French Revolution," said Candice. I shook my head.

Devonte raised his hand. "Was it the Cold War?"

"No, that came later," I said, trying not to hurl insults at them.

Ryan, who considers himself a history buff, grinned and raised his hand. "The Civil War," he said.

"Thanks, Ryan, you saved me from total despair." I wondered how many other students were unable to answer my simple question. "What makes the Gettysburg Address so famous?" I continued. "What historical documents did Lincoln refer to?"

Candice raised her hand. I feared what she would come up with. She stated, "The Declaration of Independence in the beginning and the Constitution at the end."

"Perfect, Candice. That's really impressive. What else makes it so famous?"

"It's really short," said Amanda.

"Excellent observation," I said. "He packed a lot of meaning into a few minutes, whereas Edward Everett, the speaker before Lincoln, went on for two hours."

"That was a peroration," said Devonte.

I almost fainted that he could pronounce the word and use it correctly. How could he know that, but not have a clue what war it was? I wanted to discuss the meaning of *paradox* but decided to be optimistic. "I'm pleased with your comment, Devonte. Yes, I see you're working hard for me today."

DAY 115
Game Day

On game day the basketball players are required to dress up. I suppose the tradition began to promote team spirit and a resolve for their best performance. Wow. They look nice today, yesterday's thugs transformed. They're wearing pressed khaki pants, light blue dress shirts, ties, shiny black shoes, and their navy team windbreakers. They stand tall and fit, well-groomed, and are even acting a little mellower in the classroom.

I can't believe they're the same kids as the day before. I pictured baggy jeans, underwear showing, ratty sweatshirts with hoods up concealing ear plugs and headphones, gym shoes, and, worst of all, rotten surly attitudes. Totally disengaged from my lesson, I had to correct them for texting, talking across the room to each other, and having the girls rub lotion on their arms.

Ja Quan spoke, jolting me from that sorry scene. "You comin' to our game tonight, Ms. Ball?"

"If your performance on the court is no better than what I find in the classroom, I see no reason to waste my time." But he looked so handsome I softened a bit. "But I might consider it if you start acting as nice as you look today."

DAY 116
Assimilation

Malik came to the United States three years ago from Senegal. He appeared at my desk and asked where he should sit and what assignment he needed to do. I discovered he spoke three languages, Fulani, French, and English. He became a valuable asset to the school, translating for teachers having African students who couldn't speak English. Malik had perfect attendance, impeccable manners, and never skipped an assignment.

Fast forward three years to the present, to the disgrace of American culture. I observe him wasting time in study hall, hanging with Shaq and Elijah, listening to music on his iPod, and texting. When I call him to task he scowls and says typical things like, *It wasn't me. I'm doing my work. Why you always yelling at me?* His voice has changed from soft and respectful to loud and disrespectful, imitating the inner city dialect of the cool tough guys in the school.

"I'm so disappointed with Malik," I remarked to my coworkers at lunch today. "He's not the same sweet boy who arrived here three years ago. He talks and acts like Shaq and Elijah." The others agreed. It's called *assimilation*, I was informed.

DAY 117
Waiting for Superman

Mrs. Hicks came to my room today for more babysitting. She wanted to talk about some of the kids she was having trouble with, and asked me if I was having trouble with them, too. I was highly disappointed to see her because I was waiting for a man.

Last night I went to see that education documentary called *Waiting for Superman*. It glorified charter schools and sympathized with parents in a lottery for the few coveted openings, dramatizing the devastation of those who don't draw the winning numbers. Their children are doomed for another year in neighborhood public schools.

The movie targeted failing school districts that don't fire bad teachers. At the mercy of unions, administrators shuffle the "lemons" around from one school to the next. Parents and students are "waiting for Superman" to fix what ails public education.

Charter schools in Cincinnati have not been so super. Some have been notorious for financial mismanagement and poor student performance on standardized tests. I'm waiting for Superman, too, only my image is not that of a charter school.

My superman is a stern, burly principal, highly visible throughout the building. He implements a clear discipline system and is not afraid to kick kids out who sabotage the learning of the majority. He is willing to stand up to parents and go to court for expulsion hearings, not content merely to take his six figure salary back to his home in the suburbs, with his nice wife, and children he sends to private schools.

I'm waiting for someone to magically appear in my room just as a kid is ruining my lesson. Superman will have everyone's attention and all students will know that his words have credibility and that he'll follow the discipline system as it's written.

My superman will listen to teachers and take their suggestions on attendance, grading, dress code, and discipline policies. But he won't hesitate to fire an educator not pulling his weight in the profession.

I'm not looking for a new name for a school, but a man, a superman to lead the one we have. And if he looks anything like Clark Kent, I'll give him extra credit.

DAY 118
Attending to Details

Someone keeps tearing off his fingernails and letting them drop on the floor by the computers. It's got to be a boy because no girl has nails that big. The jagged white crescents are repulsive to encounter at the end of the day when I'm straightening the desks and picking up paper, pencils, and books that students left behind. They're so gross and startling they would even turn the custodians' stomachs. So I have pity on them and pick them up myself with a paper towel, wondering what it has to do with academics. With two master's degrees and 28 years of teaching experience, I'm overqualified for the job, but someone has to do it. I suspect the gross crescents belong to Elijah, who isn't overqualified. He sits in that spot during study period and does nothing but look at his iPhone. I'm so busy helping other students I forget to spy on him. Someday when I'm free for a minute, I'll catch him in the act and demote him to do my job.

DAY 119
A-Please-Ment

It's February and I'm introducing WWII and explaining the concept of appeasement. "France and Great Britain gave in to the demands of Germany hoping Hitler would be satisfied and another world war avoided." I compared Hitler to a spoiled child throwing a tantrum in a grocery store demanding candy, while the mother, France and Great Britain, kept giving the child candy to shut him up.

I was pleased with my analogy and was sure it sparked an insightful question when Brandy raised her hand. "What time is this class over?"

Stick a pin in an inflated balloon and that was me. I looked at the calendar. "The same time it has been over since the start of school five months ago."

Leah raised her hand. "When is Martin Luther King Day?" Again, I looked at the calendar. "It was in January, weeks ago." My voice raised and cracked with annoyance. "You must have missed the day we discussed his legacy. Can we get back on topic?"

"Hitler persecuted other minorities besides Jews, like blacks," offered Brian.

"Fair enough," I said, feeling appeased enough to continue my lesson.

DAY 120
Disabled List

I have more casualties than usual this quarter. My room looks like an infirmary. Three students can't write and one can't walk. They seem happy to think they're not responsible for their grades.

Chasity dislocated her shoulder playing basketball. She'll be out for six weeks. Not just out of the games, but out of class work too, sitting there in a sling. The doctor said she's not allowed to write. I don't know how I should grade her. She's sitting next to Candice and claims they're "working together," Candice scribing. So all papers, including notebook, will have both names. Oh well, I'll crack the window and let a little integrity escape. It will be less work for me anyway.

Ethan broke his arm in gym class. I told him his notebook assignments were still due and that he could type them since the doctor's note allowed it. I remind him every day about the notebook, but he never comes to class with typed work. I'll roll with it and give him an F for his notebook grade.

Tony hurt his knee playing football. Lucky for me, he can't get out of his seat that easily. Unlucky for me, he funnels all his energy to his mouth and talks more, if that's possible. His hand is fine to write, but he never does much of that anyway.

Ja Quan broke his finger, and his hand is in a cast for three weeks. I thought I'd seen everything only to discover Maya rubbing lotion on poor "Quanny's" arm. "I don't mind you taking notes for him, Maya, but that's inappropriate and unnecessary."

"What you mean?" she snapped. "He can't do it hisself."

I made a split decision to let it go since most everyone else was on task, and the Bath and Body wasn't making noise. I'm chalking today up to broken body parts.

DAY 121
Taking Requests

My coworker Ms. Z has requested that in this illustrious collection I include her all-time favorite school story after her 29 years in the classroom.

She gave notice to Donnie, her sophomore world history student, of his skipped assignments, hoping to motivate him to salvage his grade before report cards came out. "You're failing my ass!" was his reply.

DAY 122
A Delicate Topic

The decision to let kids use the restroom is a hard call. On a scale of one to ten, ten being highest, the level of difficulty is twelve.

Requests to use the restroom come in all forms. "Man, I gotta use it," and "I gotta pee," are two of the most common. A distressed facial expression accompanied by a foul smell, and "Could I *please* use the restroom?" will get a kid out of class every time. What won't get a kid out is the one who asks every day at the same time. That smells of meeting someone for something they're not supposed to do. I make a kid sit back down who comes to my desk acting desperate, then, when given permission, stops by another student's desk to chat. "Sit down," I say, "you can't have to go that bad." The smokers and druggies have been pretty much figured out after the first quarter. The administration has put all teachers on notice—no permission to leave the room ever.

Actually, no one is permitted to leave the room without his planner. It's a handy booklet given to each student the first day of school with sections for writing assignments, pages of information such as math formulas, maps, presidents, etc., and pages of hall passes teachers are supposed to sign to allow a kid out of the room. That rule lasts about two weeks when most have lost them. Then kids stand at my desk whining and demanding to leave the room taking no responsibility for their new free planners. So, stressing accountability, I let them go provided they serve a ten minute detention with me after school. They either sit back down or walk out of class refusing to serve it. (Walking out of class without permission is highly encouraged only before vomiting.)

Every day I observe kids hanging out near their restrooms ten minutes before school or after lunch. They scurry to class when the bell rings only to interrupt me to use the restroom just when I'm starting my lesson. Then there are the girls with their women drama issues who evoke more leniencies than the boys, and on and on.

Most days I get in trouble from both sides. The administration reprimands me for students in the hallways and parents complain if I don't let their children go. "When nature calls," I'm told, "my child can't help it."

When nature calls, it's a no win situation. The restroom dilemma is a pain in the ass.

DAY 123
Affirmative Discipline

Just when I think schools need stricter discipline policies, the experts are recommending more lenient ones. Today, an article jumped out at me from the newspaper. The Obama administration is urging schools to "abandon overly zealous discipline policies." It said that although minorities account for only 15% of school population, they account for 44% of the suspensions.

It seems that Obama, Attorney General Eric Holder, and the American Civil Liberties Union are the experts, and school administrators and teachers know nothing. Do experts of all organizations reside outside of its buildings' walls? Would they dare to enter the schools and observe just who is causing disruptions? Nowhere in the article is there a statement from a current educator.

Let the experts come into the cafeterias, halls and classrooms. They might find that the minorities are the kids causing the problems and that no one is trying to suspend or expel anyone in particular.

For uneducated educators, the experts recommend training in classroom management, conflict resolution, and de-escalation of classroom disruptions. Madison has already paid tens of thousands of dollars to consultants to train school personnel on just these topics. Perhaps experts might further recommend affirmative action for discipline problems. The Obama administration could mandate that a certain quota of whites, blacks, Hispanics, etc. receive punishments regardless of who is causing the problems.

Contrary to what the experts think, when I discipline students I don't see color, I see behavior. When I come to work I'm not looking for trouble. Disruption jumps out and hits me in the face—as hard as this article just hit me.

DAY 124
Troubleshooting

For a government assignment the kids had to identify a U.S. or world problem, devise a plan of action, and tell what form of civic participation they'd use to carry out their plan. The kids chose topics such as world hunger, racial profiling, and animal abuse. I was satisfied with the fine job they did presenting their findings to the class. I decided to do some modeling for them and talked about my school stories. My presentation went thus:

Problem: Failing U.S. Schools

Explanation: A new international survey reports that Americans aren't developing as many math, science, or language skills as kids in other countries. Five thousand American students took a two hour exam called Program for International Student Assessment (PISA). It was given to 15-year-olds around the globe. Among the 65 countries that participated, the U.S. ranked 15th in reading, 23rd in science, and 31st in math. Ranking highest were the countries of Japan, China, and Thailand. U.S. Secretary of Education Arne Duncan stated we're being "out-educated" and that this is a wakeup call.

Plan of Action: I'm writing a book called *185 Days: School Stories*. Acting as a muckraker, my target is U.S. public schools. A teacher for 28 years, I give an "in the trenches" view of what it's like in a typical classroom. Through humor, I expose the problems of a weak administration, incompetent teachers, lazy and disruptive students, and burdensome state and federal mandates.

Civic Participation: I belong to a writing group called Women Writing for (a) Change (WWf(a)C) where I work on my stories and read them to a public audience. In addition, I hope to publish my manuscript. The projected completion date is fall of 2014.

I looked at the class and held up my binder of stories expecting to find the kids doodling or sleeping. Pleasantly shocked, I saw bright faces and hands raised. "Am I in it?" one after another asked. "Will you read us a story?"

"You're all in it. But I've changed names so I won't get a lawsuit, and I've fudged situations here and there," I confessed.

"Oh please read one," they begged. "We won't tell on you."

I chose a rather innocuous one from years past, not daring to target anyone in particular. The kids liked it but weren't as satisfied as if I had told a recent story and named real names. "Read us one about this class," they begged.

"Read about me," insisted Wanyé, the class troublemaker, "I know I'm in one."

I was impressed with their self-awareness and willingness to laugh at themselves. "That's enough civic participation for me," I said. "It's time to get back to our chapter."

DAY 125
No Exit

I've adopted a coworker's pat answer to hypochondriacs who ask to go to the nurse several times a week. "You don't appear to require emergency services," she says, plopping a garbage can next to their desks. "Not unless I see puke or blood."

DAY 126
Mediation

Crossing the playground on the way to the Board office, I saw two 6th graders taking swings at each other. I hurried between them. "Mark, James, there is no fighting at school."

"He said somethin' to me first," yelled Mark. "He made me."

"Are you a puppet? Do you let James pull your strings?"

"No, but he's trying to start somethin' with me."

"Well, I'm ending something," I declared. "Mark, you go sit on the bench and decide whether you're a puppet or a person. And James, you go stand by the steps and figure out if you're on a playground or a battleground. If you're both still in your *time out* places when I return, I'll see you've found the answers."

DAY 127
Blind Man's Bluff

"Tracy, please be quiet."

"It wasn't me."

"But I'm looking right at you. I can see you talking."

"I wasn't talking."

"Tracy, I can see you. This school district doesn't hire blind teachers."

DAY 128
Tired, Not Retired

I turned 65 this school year and signed up for Medicare. Do I think that's a clue I need to stop teaching? Countless people keep asking me when I'm going to retire. Is it so obvious I need to? Do I look and act that badly? Or are friends just being nice, wanting me to have more time for travel, golf, and writing. Writing? No way can I retire until I reach Day 185. If I'm not in the classroom, I won't have any material for my stories. If I try to write them post retirement, they won't be as fresh and I won't be as emotionally connected with school and the kids as I am now. But it's so hard to write and teach on the same day. I'm a morning person and the job has gotten the best of me by late afternoon and evening when I'm tired and start making excuses not to write. But if I don't teach, I won't have any subject matter. So if I want to retire, I have to write fast and often and hope the kids keep giving me something to say.

DAY 129
Plan B

James was on time for a switch. He arrived precisely at 8:00 just as I clicked *send attendance* to the office. He started unwrapping a McDonald's breakfast sandwich and set a large drink on his desk.

"Put that away," I said. "Class starts at 8, not breakfast." He took a long swig of his drink, spread out a napkin, and finished unwrapping his sandwich. "James, we're not setting up breakfast now. You eat breakfast before school."

"I ain't wastin' this," he grumbled.

"I didn't say to. Wrap it up and eat it later."

"Why are you so strict? Other teachers don't care."

"I was taught that work begins at 8, not breakfast."

"I HEARD YOU THE FIRST FIVE TIMES, Ms. Ball," he said putting the sandwich away.

I thought that remark was pretty funny and I lightened up. "This room smells like a fast food restaurant and it's making us all hungry," I said. "Tomorrow you can have your McDonald's, James, provided you bring enough for everyone."

DAY 130
Boys' Refrain

"Où Sont les Neiges d'Antan?" is the title and refrain of a French ballad written by François Villon around 1461. It means *Where are the snows of yesteryear?* A nostalgic invocation to the heroism, beauty, and power of the ladies of ancient times, the melodic line has stuck in my head ever since my college days when I studied French literature. I keep repeating it to myself when I think of certain students such as Zach, Eric, and Jacob.

I had Zach when I taught 6th grade. I picture him sitting in the middle of my class, neatly combed chestnut hair, kind intelligent face, and eyes full of life and energy. His hand was always raised, and papers perfect. He got straight A's, helped others with their work, and made up his mind to become a veterinarian.

When I was transferred to the high school, he was enrolled in my 10th grade U.S. history class. Only his seat was empty. I asked the counselor, "Where's Zach?" I got no definite answer, just some reference to alcohol, drugs, and a bad influence girlfriend. When he finally showed up, I gave him a list of missing work and a pep talk/lecture on how highly I regarded him and how it was time to get back on track for veterinary school. I just knew I'd saved him, and that he'd come to my class the next day with quality work, and start being the same good old 6th grade Zach. He didn't come back. He came here and there with a little work here and there, but not enough to pass history, earn a diploma, or go to college. I encountered dull eyes, a distracted gaze, and his head on his desk. The only thing that remained of Zach was his neatly combed chestnut hair. By third quarter he stopped coming to school altogether. My talk couldn't compete with the alcohol, drugs, and sex out there somewhere. I don't know what happened to him or where that bright boy went. *Où sont les neiges d'antan?*

Eric in my world history class was a sophisticated thinker with close cropped blonde hair and clear gray eyes that saw like a Harvard professor. He was always up for a good discussion or debate and stood at my desk after the bell to argue about the Soviets, Vietnam, or the Middle East. I knew I had to bring my A game to class or I'd lose kids like Eric.

I lost him too, to poverty. To help his mom and grandma, he worked afternoons and evenings at McDonald's. He started skipping assignments, but no big deal, he knew the material for the tests. It became a big deal when he started writing his English papers or sleeping during my class. When I called him out on it, I got grumbling and disrespect.

The year ended and I gave him a pep talk/lecture praising his unusual intelligence and begging him to apply to Saint X, a private school with high academic standards. It reserves scholarships each year for boys like Eric. He didn't apply. He was back his junior year in my French class. To my delight, he started out erect in his seat, understanding everything, and modeling written and oral responses for the rest of the class. Gradually, his head went down, sweat shirt hood over it. Often he tried to sneak in work for other classes. He became disrespectful, then absent, and then truant.

I don't know what happened to Eric, but I suspect he was introduced to alcohol and drugs during the night hours with the wrong people at work. What else could have caused such an abrupt change in behavior? Where is my thinker, my St. X grad, my *be anything you want to be* student? *Où sont les neiges d'antan?*

Jacob left Madison after his freshman year. He did go to St. X upon the insistence of his Gifted Program teacher Ms. B. He was a short pudgy kid with black hair and an exuberant innocent face. He sat alert in my world history class, always a question to enhance, not interrupt, my lecture.

Three years later some dark haired kid showed up in my senior government class. He threw himself into a desk in the back of the room and pulled a ski cap over his head. I didn't know him or like his smart alec demeanor. The kids insisted I knew him, but I had to check his schedule for his name. I was hoping he came to the wrong class and that I could send him to another room. "Jacob!" I gasped. I recognized the name but not the taller, thinner, disdainful physique.

I talked to him after class and found out he was expelled after three quarters from St. X. He went to another school, then to a home for delinquent youth, and ended up back at Madison. Today I found out he's been suspended for ten days for having alcohol in his water bottle. I don't know if he'll make it back to my class or if those dull eyes will ever be bright again. *Où sont les neiges d'antan?*

A teacher to three potentially outstanding boys, I was unable to make a difference. I can only offer an English translation of the last stanza of the French ballad:

> *Prince, don't ask me in a week*
> *or in a year what place they are.*
> *I can only give you this refrain:*
> *Where are the snows of yesteryear?*

DAY 131
Too Tardy

Tony missed his first bell senior government class altogether. He barged into the room halfway through my second bell French class asking for the work he missed.

"I'm not stopping this class to explain last class's work," I huffed. "All these kids were on time. Come back during study bell or before lunch."

He did come back, decked out in sunglasses and big red headphones. "I'm not talking to you until you remove your paraphernalia. This isn't music class, and when I came to work on time this morning, the sun wasn't out."

He put out his hand for a high five. "Gimme one, Ms. Ball, we cool, ain't we?"

Instead of a high five, I handed him his assignment. "I'll high five and be cool with you whenever or if ever you can sit in my class for an entire week from start to finish and behave and do your work." We looked at each other knowing that wouldn't happen. "When or if you graduate," I continued, "do you know how you can distinguish yourself from 90% of the work force?"

"No Ma'am."

"Show up every day on time. That's all. No employer cares about high fives or being cool. I'll know by tomorrow morning if you're ready to heed that simple advice."

DAY 132

Cliché

Today I came into my first bell government class all amped up after watching Obama's State of the Union Address the night before. When it was time for the veterans category, he pointed out a U.S. Army Ranger, Cory Remsburg, sitting in the audience between his father and the First Lady Michelle. Remsburg had served ten tours in Iraq and Afghanistan. On the most recent, he was hit by a roadside bomb and almost died. After intense rehab, he could finally see out of one eye and breathe and eat without tubes. When he is well enough, he plans to continue serving his country. Obama told his story of service, heroism, and perseverance, and, with the help of his father, the sergeant stood up to receive a two minute ovation. He had the most humble and respectful look on his face, and I sat and cried.

Full of patriotism during our opening Pledge of Allegiance, I insisted as always that everyone stand. Everyone did except Eliot. I stormed to my desk, got my clipboard, and marked an F for class participation by his name for not appreciating his country and free education.

Later I got a phone call from his father. "My son told me you failed him for the day. The Pledge of Allegiance is against our religion. Our religion is family, and we don't respect no government, nothin' except our own family."

I started to make several rebuttals: 1. Standing for the Pledge is not an unreasonable request. 2. He has stood for it other days. 3. Go live in Iran or North Korea and see how bad the U.S. is. Instead, I replied, "Thank you very much for calling. I will restore his class participation for today."

I'm sure he was expecting an argument and I disappointed him. I couldn't get off of the phone soon enough. In the luxury of my mind I indulged in a cliché, *Now I know why your son behaves as he does. The apple doesn't fall far from the tree.* Then I continued my work on less futile endeavors.

DAY 133
Seating Chart

When a new class of students comes to my room, I make them stand in the front of the room. Until I get to know their names and behaviors, I seat them from A-Z or sometimes from Z-A. Never do I let them choose their own seats, even for a minute. I want to deliver the message that this is my room and I'm in control. Otherwise, the thugs will cluster, and most others will dash for the back rows. When I get a feel for the class—it only takes a few days—I implement my strategy.

The students receive fair warning, "1. If I observe any two of you enjoying each other's company, you're separated. 2. The four worst will be spread as far apart as possible. You'll find yourselves in the four corners of the room. 3. The worst of you four will sit in the first seat in the first row nearest the door for removal purposes. 4. If you find yourself seated next to someone bad, consider I'm paying you the highest compliment since I think you're strong enough to handle it."

DAY 134
Study Hall

The world is a vampire.
I am just a rat in a cage.
— Smashing Pumpkins

Today is the first day of 4th quarter and the first day of spring. The year is three-fourths over, but I'm not slacking off. My new bulletin board quote reads, "Better the end of a thing than the beginning thereof." I want to finish the year strong. All morning I've been telling my classes that anyone can begin something, but it takes a special student to work right up to the end, in spite of the promise of spring break and summer vacation.

My optimism dissolves right after lunch during fifth bell study hall. I get all of the derelicts. They get kicked out of other classes and the guidance counselor dumps them in my room. They don't care about my board quote or working right up to vacation. Every day is a vacation for some of them—a permanent vacation from work and study.

My room is a garbage dump. I have Daniel, a rapist and drug user, Robert, a special education student who calls me "retarded," and Robby who, at the end of his sophomore year, has earned not one high school credit.

Daniel and Robby are flaming today. They saw *Brokeback Mountain* over the weekend. Robby summarizes it in a nice loud voice, "Man, it's about two gay cowboys butt fucking and stuff." He gestures and gives sound effects: "ba bum, ba bum, ba bum." I tense and become enraged. There are two sweet 7th grade girls working on their homework together. It is my responsibility to provide a healthy and quiet atmosphere for study. I am trying to get ready for the next class. I need this time. After school I spend most of my time taking care of my invalid mother and I'm not totally ready for every class first thing in the morning. I become frustrated, angry and nervous. Daniel and Robby dominate. They shout cowboy expressions back and forth across the room in a John Wayne voice. "Yippee I O Ky Yay!" Back and forth, over and over they repeat the lines, laughing and gesturing.

"Daniel and Robby, shush up and sit in your assigned seats." They ignore me. I am invisible, a nobody to them. Daniel keeps saying, "Yippee I O Ky Yay." Robby keeps saying, "Howdy, Partner." Daniel looks high. His speech and bodily movements make it obvious. I know the look. He's not in control and I'm not either.

I go to the office to tell the assistant principal that I think Daniel is high. His desk is full of pink slips and discipline referral forms. Several kids are in his office. I see he doesn't need any more problems, but I interrupt. "Daniel seems high, what do you want me to do?"

"I'll tell Mr. Howard." The principal comes to my room and gets Daniel. Daniel is out of the room for a while and Robby pipes down some. I should throw him out too, but I've thrown him out so many times this year, and the assistant principal keeps sending him back. I work for a few minutes. The principal brings Daniel back and asks me to step out in the hall.

"The last time Daniel's probation officer checked him, he was clean," says Mr. Howard. "He's checking him tonight too, so we'll just wait and see." He walks away and leaves me with Daniel and Robby.

What am I supposed to do with them in the meantime? To hell with the principal, assistant principal, and the probation officer. Daniel is high, he's in my room now, and no one is helping me. I sit down at my desk, and realize I'm not properly prepared for the next class. I feel sick and desperate. I look at the clock. Ten minutes remain. Daniel and Robby are still at it. There's no use saying anything to them and no use sending them to the office. I want to tell Daniel and Robby, "I have to live with you for ten more minutes; you have to live with yourselves for the rest of your lives. Yippee I O Ky Yay." But I don't. I would get fired for ruining their self-esteem.

I am no longer at one with the Tao, a beautiful Buddhist book I discovered. I don't practice all the good ideas that make so much sense while I'm reading in bed at night before I fall asleep. The solutions offered in the book, such as "Stop trying to control. Let go of fixed plans and concepts, and the world will govern itself," do not work for me at school.

The bell rings. study hall is over. My nerves are shot and my spirit is broken, yet I have two more classes to face before Day 134 is over. My board quote is an abstraction having nothing to do with the reality of fifth bell study hall.

DAY 135
Withholding

Jacob stands at my desk after a ten day suspension. He was caught with alcohol in his water bottle. "What did I miss?" he asks in a half grin half frown.

Annoyed, I reached for my lesson plan book trying to recall the past two weeks of government work. Then I remembered my new rule for students who have missed multiple days of school. I pulled one paper from my folder. "Here, Jacob, read chapter 8 and answer these questions. When I get this back I'll give you the next thing."

It used to take me over a half hour assembling and writing down assignment after assignment, only to get nothing back or finding the kid absent or in trouble again.

"But I want to have everything I missed," he protested.

"This is fair play," I said. "You turn in this first, and I'll gladly have chapter 9 ready for you tomorrow."

DAY 136
I'm Salty

My fourth bell class always falls apart ten minutes before lunch. The seniors get to leave early, so four privileged ones get up at 11:44 whether I'm finished with my lesson or not. The rest of the students cut me off mid sentence too. I'd love to spend that time reviewing or having kids start their homework. But since everyone has decided not to listen to me anymore, I sit at my desk and eavesdrop on their conversations. I might find out what they're interested in and figure out a way to connect it to something I'm teaching.

"I was so salty this morning," I heard Brittany say.

"What does salty mean?" I asked. I'd heard that word used in the hallways. It sounded like it had something to do with sex, and if it did maybe I shouldn't have asked.

"Oh you know Miz Ball, like if you found out your husband was cheatin' on you, you'd be salty," said Brittany. "Like I'm salty 'cause Tommy stole my iPod and Dr. McKee didn't do nothin' about it."

"So, salty means you're indignant or outraged," I said.

"I don't know what them words mean, but they sound alright."

"Like you're shocked and pissed and have an attitude all at the same time," explained Kendra.

"That's pretty comprehensive," I said. "I don't know of any conventional word that covers all of those feelings. Thanks for telling me about salty."

"No problem, Miz Ball, and you pronounce it *saldy*." They laughed and dashed from the room as the lunch bell rang.

The next day I was struggling with that class trying to squeeze in as much information as possible before the Ohio Graduation Test. "You're going to have to know the standard on Civil Rights. Who can name the four changes in voting rights during the 20th century? Kendra, put the photos away. Brittany, go to your assigned seat."

"Oh whatever," said Brittany as she got up.

Kendra threw the pictures into her purse. "Whatever floats your boat, Miz *Balls.*"

"It seems I'm the only one taking the OGT seriously, and I have *my* high school diploma."

"See Miz Ball, you be so salty right now," said Kyla.

"Brush the salt off your shoulder," said James.

I breathed in and got ready to lash out a command to go to the office. But I couldn't send all four of them. I breathed out and looked at all the defiant and mischievous faces. A smile formed on the corner of my mouth. The kids noticed it before I could put back my serious face. "Look, Miz Ball's laughing!" I laughed outright and the kids were delighted. "See, ain't it fun when you're not so salty all the time?"

"Maybe, but the superintendent will get salty with me if you all don't pass the test."

"Don't worry, we know this stuff," said Brittany. "The changes in voting in the 20th century are the 19th Amendment, the Voting Rights Act, the 24th Amendment, and the 26th Amendment."

"Sweet," I said.

DAY 137
Paper Plethora

I pass out the notebook guide for chapter 10 and repeat my standard paper lecture. "These are the activities for the whole chapter. I only ran enough handouts for one per person. Don't lose yours. You're not going to get another one. The school can't afford paper and ink for five copies of everything for every student. Everyone is here today, so I know you all got one."

The next day I say, "Get out your chapter 10 notebook guide and we'll work on activity 10.2."

"Do you have an extra?" asks Shaq. "Mines at home."

"Can I have one?" says Devonte. "Mines in my locker."

"I need one," whines Samantha. "Mines in Miss Cook's room."

I'm ready to kill myself. This goes on six bells a day for every handout. "If I give you another today, you'll still need another tomorrow. This school can't afford your irresponsibility," I cry. "I know you all got a copy yesterday."

So I face the familiar dilemma. Do I let them sit there idle and disrupt class, or do I dole out more copies, ruin my credibility, and perpetuate the paper plethora?

The kids broke me down all the time until I broke myself of my sugar addiction. If there was candy in the house, I'd eat it. Now, I really don't have any more copies because I don't run more.

"Sorry," I say, "one per person. Do the work when you find your own paper. For now, just read the section in your book. Maybe tomorrow you'll care enough to bring it to class."

DAY 138
Silent Majority/Deafening Minority

Vilfredo Pareto, an Italian economist, says 20% of your work consumes 80% of your time and resources. Pareto's Principle can be applied to public education as well as business.

While reading the introduction to chapter 36 on the Vietnam War to 20 students during seventh bell, Eric fell asleep over his open text. "Get your head up," I said. A big pool of drool lay in the middle of a picture of President Johnson with his head on his desk in the Oval Office. Johnson had just heard a taped report of the Tet Offensive. The kids sitting around Eric made noises showing that they were grossed out. I handed him a paper towel. "That's a $20 fine. That book was brand new when issued to you. Would you want to touch that page if someone else had done that?" Eric grinned, shut the book, and lay his head back down. I was as exasperated with this class as Johnson was with the Vietnam War.

"Glue your maps of the Ho Chi Minh Trail at the top of your notebook page and answer the questions that go with it. We're going to explore how the Viet Cong transported weapons to South Vietnam." Darrell was out of his seat and roamed to the window sill for Kleenex. I heard him call Robby a fag. "Darrell, sit down," I said, determined to defuse all negative situations.

"You ain't see what Robby just did? You always gettin' me in trouble."

"Just sit down," I said.

"But that ain't fair. You always yellin' at me."

"This isn't a discussion. Go to the office. You weren't in trouble until you started arguing."

Darrell took his time leaving, stopping to get hand sanitizer and the attention of the others. They accommodated him with noises of approval, forgetting their maps and questions.

"Get to work," I said. "In 20 minutes we'll discuss how U.S. efforts were undermined by the secret trail. I circulated around the room giving clues to answers and making sure the glue sticks worked. "Put that magazine away," I whispered to Daniel. He ignored me so I chose to deal with him after school.

As I bent over to help Chasity, the first row exploded. "Oh, not again," several students yelled. Devin was out of his seat, jumping and holding his nose. "Jeremy farted," he announced. "Can I sit in the back?" The last time that happened everyone ran either out the door or to the windows and the rest of the time was wasted.

"No, sit down," I said. "I'll open the windows and spray some air freshener. Get back to work." Austin clasped his hand over his mouth and glued his eyes to his book.

Devin got right in my face. "I ain't sittin' next to him."

"Sit down," I insisted. "You need to practice some social skills."

"Shut up," he told me and threw his pencil across the room. I wished I had some Agent Orange to spray on him.

"Go to the office," I told him, hating to add to its load.

I looked at the class impressed with those mature and motivated enough to keep on task. "Let's refocus. We'll review the assignment in five minutes." Desiree and Terrace were already finished and working on the bonus questions. I went to my desk to collect myself and write Devin's referral.

By the time class ended, I had completed one-fourth of the work that I had planned for the students. I was enraged that 20% of the students consumed 80% of the resources both in the classroom and in the office, knowing that this happens in most classrooms most days with no effective system in place to stop it. I was sad for those held hostage by the disruption, and baffled that the administration can't embrace a simple concept known as Pareto's Principle.

The next day I told the class that Johnson did not run for a second term. His vision of a Great Society was blurred by the war. Nixon was elected as protests against Vietnam became violent. His administration coined the term *Silent Majority.* I wrote it in big letters on the board. "They were the middle class voters weary of the social upheaval of the 1960s. They were called the forgotten Americans, the non-shouters, the non-demonstrators." I paused to glare at Eric, Darrell, Daniel, and Devin. "Write the definition in your notebooks and brainstorm how that definition could apply to your own experiences right here at school."

DAY 139
Newsworthy

News article for the *Madison Journal*:

Silent Majority

Silent majority is a political term dating from the 1960s during the Nixon administration. The silent majority represented the middle class voters who were weary of the protests and social upheaval of the Vietnam War. They were called the "forgotten Americans, the non-shouters, the non-demonstrators."

This term can be applied to a school as well as a country. There's a silent majority of students right here at Madison High School. They're the ones who come to school every day on time, prepared, and who follow the rules. They don't call attention to themselves or waste valuable instruction time getting detentions, office referrals, In School Discipline, or suspensions.

Although silent, they are not forgotten. Lori Schilling, Milan Rogers, Sally Turner, Samantha Harper, Jessica Hopkins, and Andrew Kelly are great examples. They don't have to be told to be quiet or tuck in their shirts. They have their books, notebooks, pens, and assignments. They sit patiently while the teachers deal with the noise makers.

These and many other students draw attention to themselves where it counts—on paper. Their quality work speaks for itself. They're the producers, not consumers of energy drained from classroom instruction.

Thank you, members of the silent majority. Although you may not realize it, teachers hear you loud and clear and appreciate your positive contributions to Madison High School. We will see you on the honor roll, in college envelopes announcing scholarships, and on stage at the awards assembly.

DAY 140
Notes

I love notes and get high confiscating them. I use them to embarrass the kids, to blackmail them, and as a teaching opportunity. My classes receive fair warning at the beginning of the year. "If I see you writing, reading, or passing notes, I'll take them and do what I please with them. Anything of yours I don't see is none of my business, but if I see something out other than your work, it's no longer your property."

If it's a love note, I may read it out loud to mortify someone who likes someone. I took this yellow post-it note from Ashley. *I can swear Brian looks cuter and cuter every day. I just wanna walk right up to him and kiss him.*

I use them for blackmail by threatening to show their parents if there is another incident of misbehavior. I took away a drawing of a lewd sex act from Wayne. I didn't punish him right away. He constantly disrupted class so I had to think of something good. "Do you want your mom to see this?"

"No."

"Then if you even breathe wrong, I'll show it to her." I had Wayne wrapped around my little finger for the rest of the year.

I save notes for parent-teacher conferences. They provide me with solid evidence when a parent tries to blame me for the child's failing grade. "No Sir, it's not me. Your child is not doing what she's supposed to. She's doing this instead." And I show him the note. The name and handwriting can't be denied.

I seize the opportunity for a teachable moment, especially in language arts class. I use notes to correct grammar, spelling, and punctuation errors, using the kids' own sentences that are more amusing than the ones in the book.

Example 1: A. *Ha, Ha, you don't have a girl no more.*

             B. *Who give a crap*

Correction: "It's *any* more, *gives,* and a question mark goes at the end of the sentence."

Example 2: A. *Hi, Hon, wat up wit u?*

             B. *nothing Im fucking board*

Correction: "What is *w-h-a-t,* not *w-a-t.* There's an apostrophe between the *I* and the *m* in *I'm,* and *bored* is spelled *b-o-r-e-d,* not *b-o-a-r-d.*

Example 3: A. *I'm board, how bout you*

             B. *Yea, I wish I was at home. I'm so tired!*

             A. *Yeah, me to… plus my nipple hurts*

             B. *Oh? Didn't need ta no dat one*

Correction: "The feeling bored is *b-o-r-e-d,* not the wooden *b-o-a-r-d.* You say *I wish I were at home,* not *was.* It's *t-o-o,* meaning also, not *t-o.* And it's *k-n-o-w,* not *n-o.* I write all this on the *b-o-a-r-d.*

A whole world exists underneath the subject I happen to be teaching at the time. The kids are involved in so much personal drama, it's no wonder they're not paying attention to my flimsy lesson.

Example 1: A. *When was the last time you sucked a dick*

I intercepted that one before the reply.

Example 2: A. *I got a question. Is Amy pregnant?*

             B. *No, Brittany started it and blamed it on me and you heard what Amy said.*

             A. *No, wat she say*

             B. *She told me on the phone that Brittany started a rumor that*

Daniel and her "did it."

A. *Gotcha. Well she ain't pregnant. I no that for sure. But I don't think her and Daniel "did it" either. She would of told me. She tell me everything.*

Example 3: A. *Hey, I need your help. If you were tired of living with your mom but you loved her very much, how would you tell her that! Please help me.*

B. *just say "Mom I love you verey much but I wanna live with Dad. Now. You can see me on the weekends! Every weekend. I promise!"*

A. *I know. I planned and thought of that but he wouldn't be able to buy me school stuff and he would never be able to pay my doctor bills.*

Example 4: A. *I fricken board. So wat you up to? Why did Ash go home? Ok, who all goin to Destiny's party? I need a boyfriend but nobody will go with me cause I fat and ugly so that's why I don't have a b/f.*

B. *She said she was dizzy. I don't know who's going besides Ash. That ain't true! Lindsey is fat and ugly. U way better and I ain't trying to be gay. Have you asked Pat out?*

The kids have caught on to me. They know I feel powerful and smug with a note in my possession. Sometimes they put me in my place by passing decoy notes. I tear them open like a hungry wolf only to read, *Hi, Ms. Ball!* or *Ha, Ha, nothing here!*

Today I thought I had a nice juicy one. I snatched it off of Paige's desk during first bell. "Hey, Ms. Ball, that's mine!" the unruly 7th grader protested.

"Not any more," I said. Paige seldom paid attention in class or did her homework. Between classes she yelled and chased boys in the hall. I couldn't wait until class was over so I could read it in private. I just knew it was written to some boy to arrange a time and place after school for them to "do it." I was planning on either blackmailing her to get her to behave or showing it to her mom right away to prevent a preteen pregnancy.

During my planning period I settled into my comfortable desk chair and took Paige's note from my pocket. It was folded into eighths and the outside was addressed to Lele. I was disappointed because Lele was a girl, but I was sure she was telling her something she did or was going to do with a boy. I opened the note and read:

Dear Lele,

Hey girl, what you doing a week after easter cuz I babysittin and wanted to know if you wanted to go. It going to be at my mom's friend's house her name is Stephanie. Its Stephanie's 30th birthday and they paying me to watch their kids. And if you go I'll split it with you but if you don't want to its cool. You still my sister for life. Love ya lots.

Pay Pay

The innocence and sweetness of that note took the wind out of me. What a bully I was. In the future I'll confiscate notes with less confidence. Juicy, sad, funny, decoy, or simply innocuous, I'll open the next one at my own risk.

DAY 141
Little Bits

After lunch Wanyé entered my study bell called Academic Intervention (AE). Students are supposed to be working or seeking help from a teacher. He had a small open bag of Cheetos that he proceeded to spill all over the floor. "Pick them up," I said, and continued helping Leah with her French.

"I can't pick them up," he barked, then settled into talking to his buddies.

Distracted from Leah, I walked to his desk. "Turn the music off, and please pick up the Cheetos before they get stepped on."

"I told you, I can't pick them up. They too many."

"Yes you can, pick them up."

"I ain't pickin' them up."

"You're not leaving here until you do."

"I ain't touchin' them. Can I get a broom and dust pan from the custodian?"

"No, it's better to pick them up than sweep them on this type of carpet."

"I'm gettin' a broom."

"No you're not. Just go to the office. I've had enough."

Wanyé left the room and I picked up the Cheetos while the kids watched. Then I got an office referral and wrote: *Refusal to pick up a spilled snack. Defiance/disrespect/continued arguing after a simple request.*

On my way to the office, Wanyé and Mrs. Stein, the Dean of Students in charge of discipline, were coming toward me with a broom and dust pan. "Mrs. Ball," she said, "I told Wanyé he could use these."

"Mrs. Stein, I told him he couldn't. He's perfectly capable of picking up his own mess by hand. I don't want him dragging the Cheetos with a broom.

This whole thing could have been avoided if Wanyé had done what I asked in the first place."

They both ignored me and continued on to my room with the broom and dust pan. "That's not necessary," I yelled. "I picked them up myself. It took all of 30 seconds."

I was enraged with Mrs. Stein for not supporting me. "This is all about a student following a simple direction after a simple mistake," I told her. "I'm embarrassed by the pettiness of all this." I handed her Wanyé's office referral.

"Man," he said to her, "will you get me out of her AE?"

I went back to my room to help Leah, hoping Mrs. Stein would again support Wanyé's request.

DAY 142
Unprepared

I had one of my recurring nightmares last night. The theme is school and not being prepared. This dream always comes in late August when school is about to start and I'm super anxious about getting ready, and then it repeats itself throughout the year.

The dream takes many forms. My class is lined up on the playground at 8 a.m. waiting for me to lead it into the building. I have no clothes on, my hair isn't washed, and I can't find my shoes. Sometimes I dream I'm facing parents sitting in my room for Open House and I don't have a presentation. The most common dream is one of pure chaos. There are 50 students to teach and I have no lesson prepared, no worksheets run off, and no notes on the overhead to show. I try writing a sentence on the board to focus the class but it's happening in slow motion and I can't seem to finish it. But what's progressing is shouting, flying objects, and moving bodies.

Last night I dreamed I had to make a speech in the auditorium in front of administrators, teachers, parents, and students. I was supposed to talk about Gandhi. I had a long yellow legal pad with my original speech. I frantically leafed through the pages, crossing out sentences, adding some, but it still wasn't coherent. Five minutes before curtain, I discarded it and started writing a new one. Just as I was waking up, I knew how I was going to present Gandhi to the audience.

As a history teacher, my favorite topic is the Indian Independence Movement. Gandhi overthrew the British Empire in India without a single weapon. His tactics of civil disobedience and nonviolence were models for Caesar Chavez and Martin

Luther King here in America. Gandhi influenced the course of world history through skill rather than force, calling upon his keen intelligence and knowledge of law. There is no way I can adequately speak for this extraordinary man. I will use his own words, bringing him to you live, reading his famous quotes, and letting him speak for himself.

When teaching his followers about nonviolence he said,

"I am prepared to die, but there is no cause for which I am prepared to kill."

"An eye for an eye makes the whole world blind."

To temper the ardor of Hindus and Muslims he preached religious tolerance.

"I believe in the fundamental truth of all great religions."

"God has no religion."

I fully awoke leaving a waiting audience and unfinished speech, my typical dream of frustration and nonattainment.

Contrary to these types of dreams, I'm over prepared in real life. For a talk, I'm ready days in advance. In college I had my research papers written a week before the due date. Now I have stacks of extra worksheets, questions, crosswords, and word searches ready for the kids in case the computers crash, the copier breaks down, someone steals the projector from my room, or there's 10 minutes left of class and I don't want to start a new topic. In spite of my good habits, insanity sprang forth today in the classroom, and my preparations were as futile as my dream.

And what does Gandhi have to do with it? He was assassinated by a Hindu fanatic because he preached acceptance of all religions. He died by violence and religious intolerance, the opposite of two ideals he exemplified. His life should have ended peacefully sleeping in his bed.

Unable to decide how to end Day 142, I'll have Gandhi speak for dreams, school, and his own life. "Satisfaction lies in the effort, not in the attainment, full effort is full victory."

DAY 143
Save Yourself

After my sophomore French class, Danielle lingered at my desk until the room emptied. "Madame," she began in a troubled voice, "you teach the seniors government and they have to do community service, right?"

"Right."

"See, I'm really upset about world hunger and there's this UNICEF program and do you think we could start an organization here at school and collect canned goods and have fundraisers and stuff?"

My desk was cluttered with papers to grade and I still had to put an interesting lesson together because the principal was coming in later to observe me. "Danielle, I can't even get the seniors to turn in their own work, without an undertaking like that. Go to your next class and let me think about it."

There wasn't much to think about. No way was I going to take on an additional project with the kind of students I have.

Danielle is the cream of the crop at Madison. She has a 4.0 grade average, brings enthusiasm and creativity to every assignment, and is respectful and kind to teachers and peers. Unfortunately, she's one of seven children, and from a low income household. Her request was so sincere that I didn't want to discourage this exceptional girl. All evening I deliberated about how I would respond to her.

The next day I told her to hang back after class. "Danielle," I said, "I admire your desire to solve a great social problem, but that is not your job. Right now your job is to be a student, graduate as valedictorian, earn a scholarship, and go to college. You can't save the world when you're without credentials and poor. You must save yourself first. You can save it more effectively from a position of wealth and status, with higher education and a good job. Have you ever heard of Bill Gates and Warren Buffett? They're billionaires who set up foundations for world hunger, disease, and illiteracy all over the world. They have power and prestige. They are in a position to save the world, you're not. When you have your college education and a lucrative job, you can join or create charitable foundations."

After my lecture, I gave her a quiz. "What's your job?"

"To save myself."

"How?"

"Get good grades, get a scholarship, and go to college."

"Exactly. You passed."

Danielle looked as though a heavy burden had been lifted from her. She left the room much lighter and happier than I've ever seen her. I was light and happy too, for I not only saved Danielle but I saved myself.

DAY 144
With His Blessing

Mr. Blessing is our new superintendent this year. Before he started, he invited each teacher to a private meeting to "pick their brains" about the strengths and weaknesses of the school, their experiences, and welcomed suggestions for improvement. I accepted and made an appointment. Wow, I thought, this is the first time any superintendent has ever wanted to listen to what a teacher has to say.

I told him the school was so small it ought to run like a military academy, and that misbehavior should be minimal. Students get small class sizes and individual attention. However, the school falls far short of its potential. I made several points.

1. The dress code is not clear and is open to too many choices and interpretations of clothing. Either have a uniform or not.

2. There are no consequences for tardies or absences. At least one third of the students are 10-20 minutes late for school each day, and many miss 12 days a quarter with no consequence.

3. There is no solid discipline system. Repeat offenders circulate around detentions, in school discipline, and suspensions instead of a progression from bottom to top then out.

4. There is no academic vision, Ds being perfectly acceptable. Theoretically, a student could get an A 1st quarter, fail the rest of the year, and still pass the course. We used to have a policy that students must pass the 4th quarter to pass the course, preventing apathy and discipline problems in April and May.

Mr. Blessing listened and made notes on the points I made. I left his office optimistic, thinking this year would be different and teachers would get administrative support to "crack down" on the student body.

We're well into the third quarter and nothing has changed. In fact, things are worse this year. Madison took in a few thugs expelled from a neighboring school who are allowed to run the place. They cause trouble in the classrooms, halls, cafeteria, and even at sporting events. When I send them to the office because it's impossible to teach with them in the room, there is no consequence. The superintendent is too weak to stand up to them and the disruption goes on day after day.

I rarely see Mr. Blessing. He makes a brief appearance at faculty meetings, makes a few politically correct statements, and is gone. I can count on one hand the number of times he's been visible in the halls or classrooms. He either doesn't know what goes on, doesn't want to know, doesn't care, or knows and hides from reality in the Board office.

Today there was a light rap on the door during my fifth bell French class. I was shocked to look up and see Mr. Blessing. He was half in and half out of my room, as though, if he ventured any further, he'd step on a land mine. I stood to greet him and he handed me a Russell Stover solid milk chocolate candy bar. A fancy tag was attached reading *Happy Valentine's Day*. I thanked him graciously, put the candy on my desk, and resumed teaching.

Later I wanted to reply, *Mr. Blessing, that was a nice way to show teacher appreciation, but I can buy my own candy bar. I can buy myself 100 candy bars. I would rather have solid attendance, discipline, and academic policies. Those are the things I need you for, things I can't do by myself.* I realized I wasted my time at that initial meeting, and, resigned to the system, I ate the candy.

DAY 145
Overnight Success

Teachers in the elementary grades at Madison struggled to prepare their classes for the March Proficiency Tests, Brad, a 6th grade teacher included. His teaching wasn't unusually dynamic or creative and his classroom wasn't decked out with posters, inspirational quotes, or a class roster with rows of achievement stars. But he did his job and was a calm and kind presence in the school. When his students didn't do well on the standardized tests, no one held it against him. No one's class at Madison scored well. Even Miss Flynn, creative and dynamic with a decked out room, had low percentages. On average, scores came in 5% accelerated, 35% passing/proficient, and 60% basic/limited. Madison had little to brag about.

Brad got a job at another school. During his first year there his class scored 60% accelerated, 35 % proficient, and only 5% basic or limited. Wow! What a great teacher Brad was according to the test results. What did he do over the summer to prepare himself for such success?

1. Most of his students come from two parent homes.
2. They get a healthy dinner and a good night's sleep.
3. There are books, computers, and printers in their rooms.
4. The family average income is between $100,000- $200,000.
5. Moms and Dads read to their children at a young age.
6. Parents speak proper English.
7. Students have experiences such as plays, concerts, museums, and vacations to Boston, Washington D.C., and Gettysburg.

He simply changed schools.

DAY 146
How Did They Do It Without You?

It started in the early 1990s. Teachers were no longer trusted to teach their subjects of expertise and students were no longer capable of learning from them. Federal and state governments seized control of education.

Ohio began with the Proficiency Test that later became the Ohio Graduation Test. Teachers were given a manual of standards to teach and they'd better be taught. Students would be tested on them, their scores published, schools ranked, and jobs at risk. Under achieving schools were threatened and even more regulations were imposed.

Companies capitalized on their demise selling test preparation workbooks such as *Buckle Up* and *Buckle Down*. Computer software companies entered the game offering schools programs such as *Study Island, Vantage, Battelle for Kids*, and *Thinkgate*.

The joy of teaching a unit such as World War I was annihilated. Instead of including essential note taking, then a lively reenactment of trench warfare, slides or power point, then the movie or novel, *All Quiet on the Western Front*, some artwork depiction of the era, and a written reflection on the "lost generation," etc., the topic was watered down to whatever the Content Standard manual said to teach and what would be tested. The history teacher hurried to "cover" each period in order to be ready for the test date. Anxiety and preoccupation with scores, replaced a deep learning experience.

For over 20 years the teacher in-services have been a treadmill of "experts" training staff on curriculum mapping, Academic Content Standards, Common Core Standards, and Student Learning Objectives. They preach ad nauseam about formative and summative assessments, differentiating instruction, tracking progress, data, accountability, and on and on. Each year, new miracle programs arise such as ROAR, FIP, TESA, and DASL, promising to solve what ails public education. Does anyone know or care what the letters stand for? It's all too tedious and boring to elaborate, and this is only a small fraction of the buzz words.

Students are reduced to columns, rows, categories, scores, and percentages on a spread sheet. Teachers are forced to spend more time on their computers documenting student growth than interacting with their students. There's no time to arrange the desks into opposing rows of Allied and German forces and have kids hurl rubber ammunition to each other across "no man's land."

If kids weren't achieving 20 years ago, they're doing worse now. The goal of "No Child Left Behind" was to have every child on grade level by 2014. That didn't happen. It wouldn't take a genius to realize that some children will never be on grade level no matter what the program, and that some kids will be far above grade level without it.

I have a set of test questions for the politicians, education experts, or whoever out there is responsible for torturing teachers and students.

1. How did Ernest Hemingway write *For Whom the Bell Tolls* without passing a proficiency test?

2. Where did the Beatles album *Abbey Road* come from without *Study Island?*

3. How were the *Iliad* and *Odyssey* conceived without curriculum mapping?

4. How could Jane Austen possibly have written her six major novels without following the Common Core Standards?

5. What were the academic content standards in science when Edison invented the light bulb?

6. How did the innovations of Bill Gates and Steve Jobs so profoundly impact culture and business practices without formative and summative assessments?

7. Did Vincent van Gogh's teachers track his data while he painted *Starry Night*?

Their jobs will hang on their scores that will be published online and in the newspaper. I suspect results as low as those they're so arrogantly assuming to raise.

DAY 147
Discipline Fix

It's 7:50 a.m. The halls are a sea of shouting kids wearing hoodies, ear buds, and headphones. They're holding iPhones, large drinks, and bags of breakfast sandwiches. They enter 8:00 a.m. class with everything but pens and pencils, books, notebooks, and completed assignments. Eliot won't stand for the Pledge of Allegiance. Maya and Tony are hanging all over each other. "Go to your assigned seats," I demand. They ignore me. "Get out," I shout to the lovers. I begin the day at my desk writing two office referrals. I look around for a reliable student to run the form to the office. Slim pickings. I settle for Donnie.

"I don't have a pencil," whines Brady, long white cords hanging from his ears.

"Can I go to my locker and get my book?" asks Devin who's been standing at his locker since 7:30.

Then Cheyenne cries, "My homework's at my grandma's house."

I'm upset. Minutes have been wasted. Now I'm supposed to teach about the House of Representative procedures facing an unfocused and unprepared class. It's oppressive.

Help someone, anyone! I've matched today's lesson with number 17 of the Common Core Standards for government. I've mapped my curriculum, rearranged the seating chart, and documented scores. Still, I can't teach.

Does anybody get it? It's not that hard. Implement a firm discipline system and stick to it. Five *detentions* go to an *in school discipline*. Five of those result in a *suspension*, then a three day, five day, ten day, then out. It only has to happen to two or three kids at the most, and the rest will get the message.

Kick a few kids out. The world will not end. Teaching could possibly begin. Now, nothing less than assault with a deadly weapon will end in expulsion, not even alcohol, tobacco or drugs. The kids know it. So the disruption and disrespect play on and on day after day.

Schools don't need more money, materials, or innovations. I have more ideas and materials in my room than time to use them. We need rules, order, discipline, consequences, and support from principals, superintendents, and board members.

In this vast country with millions of sharp intellects, why has no one figured out what's wrong with our schools? I have discipline to sell and it's free of charge.

DAY 148
What Did You Say?

After lunch we're in study bell. It's called Academic Enrichment or AE. Most of the kids listen to music, look at their iPhones, or talk. The period would better be called Academic Emergency if an outsider peaked into the room. Even the students that I know have work to do (because I assigned it) refuse to do it. It's impossible to control their toys or force them to task.

A few good students make use of the time, and a few even ask for help. Today I was going over a French lesson with Julie when music coming from Shaq's desk made it impossible to concentrate. "Shaq, please turn that down," I called over to him. "We're trying to work." The rapping continued and I saw his big red ear-phoned head keeping the beat. I walked over to him. "Turn it down," I shouted. He looked at me in innocent wonder, head still in time with the music. I got as close to him as I dared. "Shaq, turn it off. We're trying to work!"

"What? I can't hear you," he scowled, earphones firmly affixed.

DAY 149
Whistle Blower

I'm not a phys-ed teacher but I carry a whistle. It's more useful to me than my computer. I don't use it to begin or stop a play, but to enable myself to call class to order. I blow it loud and long. The kids make fun of me, but if I use it only so often, it does shock them into a brief enough silence to squeeze in enough of a hook to begin my lesson.

Today it came in handy when Shaq wouldn't remove his headphones and turn off his music. I got right next to him and blew my whistle loud and long. My 75¢ gadget proved a formidable rival to his $400 Beats.

DAY 150
Napoleonic Code

Choosing my last question for Friday's current events, I ran across an article by columnist David Ignatius entitled "Putin Making His Mistakes." He cited Napoleon who, during an 1805 battle, cautioned, "Whenever the enemy is making a false movement, we must take good care not to interrupt him." He was referring to Putin's recent invasion of Crimea, possibly creating worse troubles the more he tries to resurrect the Soviet Union. I thought Napoleon's quote extremely clever as I set the lesson aside to face my first class of the day.

I was hurrying to wrap up our work on how a bill becomes a law so I could devote the whole next day to current events. Five minutes remained of class and I had a few more points to drive home. "Markus, please be quiet. This is the fourth time you've interrupted me."

"Ain't nobody listen' to you," was his response.

His insolence enraged me but I decided to drop it since he'd be leaving the room shortly. However, he made his second false move dropping a giant cola in the doorway just as the bell rang. I was further enraged since drinks are forbidden and I'd warned him on many occasions. "Clean it up," I said handing him a roll of paper towels, "then hurry to your next class."

Fifteen minutes later Markus reappeared in my room. "I need Stephanie to open her locker for me," he demanded. His girlfriend sitting in my French class was more than eager to follow him out of the room.

"No," I said, "she's not going anywhere, and you're supposed to be in your second bell."

I motioned him to leave when he yelled, "You're fuckin' pissing me off."

I kept silent and looked at him. "Never interrupt your enemy when he is making a mistake," I thought.

I went to the door and held it open for him. "You're a bitch," he called as I shut the door. I jotted down Markus' rhetoric and returned to my French students who were not at all disappointed by the interruption.

Later I documented Markus' behavior and took the referral to the office. It was considerably more substantial than had I written it after his first insult. He received a two day suspension and wasn't in class the next day. Unfortunately he missed the benefit of my lesson on Ignatius, Napoleon, and Putin.

DAY 151
Disarmed

Early this morning a slight man wearing paint splattered jeans came to my room. He held out his hand and introduced himself as Markus' dad. He wanted to know what happened yesterday. I gave him the blow by blow account expecting to be interrupted and fully expecting him to defend his son. He just stood there and listened. "I'm sorry," he said when I finished. "He wasn't raised like that."

In disbelief I replied, "Thank you for your support. I wasn't expecting a savior to appear."

"I see he's been suspended," he said. "I'll take care of Markus at home." He shook my hand again and rushed off to work.

It's a rarity I receive backing from both parent and administration, let alone at the same time. Feeling totally disarmed is a good way to start the day.

DAY 152
Parlez-Vous Français?

Stewart usually sleeps during my French class. I overlook it because he's a big senior mixed in with underclassmen and needs the elective credit for graduation. He does just enough work to pass with a D.

Today he sat up long enough to grumble, "What will I ever need French for?"

"Stewart," I replied, "you might meet a beautiful French woman and wish you'd have paid better attention in here. You could have impressed her with your French and flattered her with some amorous expressions. Just go back to sleep and let someone else win the lovely lady."

Stewart sat up straight. "How do you say, *will you go out with me, you're hot* and *I love you?*"

I grinned and said, "Expressions and pronunciations will be revealed to those awake enough to learn."

DAY 153
Two Different Masters

I'm Catholic and I love the Bible stories but I don't always follow the teachings. Today I'm making out third quarter grades and calculate that of 38 days, Elijah was absent 8 and tardy 14. The days he came to class he was unprepared. Robby, on the other hand, was in class every day, on time, with his work.

So what about the parable of the workers in the vineyard, Matthew 20: 1-16? The master paid all the workers a day's wage whether they worked the full day or not. The ones hired first in early morning were given a denarius and ones hired in the middle and at the end of the day received the same. The all-day workers complained but the master claimed he was being fair and was free to be as generous as he chose. "The last shall be first and the first shall be last," said he.

I'm the master of first bell senior government. Does Elijah deserve the same grade as Robby? What would happen to Robby's morale and the quality of his work if I gave them both Bs? In my vineyard Robby gets an A and Elijah gets a D. I choose to be generous to those with a work ethic. I say, "The first shall be first and the last shall be last."

DAY 154
Among the Thorns

The Bible teaches forgiveness, unconditional love, and reconciliation. I didn't follow that either today. As usual, Tony came late to class, set his book bag on his desk, and disappeared. Fifteen minutes later he returned with a Twix, Snickers, M&Ms, and headphones. He prowled around the room talking and giving high fives to his brothers, ignoring me and my lecture. I plodded through my lesson plan angry and on edge, knowing if I kick too many kids out, I'm accused of not making class interesting enough.

When the bell mercifully rang, Tony held out his fist for me to bump as best buddies. "No," I said, "I don't feel like it."

"Come on, Ms. Ball, show me a little love." He smiled as though he'd been a perfect student and locked his eyes into mine as if to control me.

"That's an empty gesture," I said keeping my hands at my side. Forgiveness implies a lesson learned and behavior changed. Tony has disrupted class since day one and will continue until day 185.

I prefer Matthew 13: 4–9. Jesus said don't waste time throwing seeds on rocky soil or among the thorns. Wait for receptive soil. I turned from Tony to prepare for the incoming class.

DAY 155
Testing 1-2-3 to Infinity

Tomorrow we have to take our students to the computer lab for more testing. We pre-tested them the first week of school on Student Learning Objectives tied to teacher evaluation. In January we had a week of semester exams. Then the kids took the Ohio Graduation Test in March tied to whether or not they receive their high school diploma. It seems the Department of Education is always trying to scare someone. In April we have to give a post test from the initial pre-test to show scores have raised enough to prove a whole year of student growth in the subject taught. These results are tied to teacher evaluation, promotions, raises, and demotions. I haven't figured out what's in this one for the students. The SLOs pull teachers away from them and to their own computers to fill in templates and document percentages. A whole year's growth? How does instruction from September through March, minus four weeks of testing, minus eight snow days constitute a whole year's worth of learning? Then there's an EOY, an end of the year test, at the end of May we're required to give, topped off with a week of second semester exams in June. The state is so fascinated with data analysis it fails to realize the kids are being tested on material teachers have no time to teach.

DAY 156
Out of Touch

Today's teaching is being disrupted for yet more testing. This is in addition to what was discussed on Day 155, and most absurd of all. Students are taking a field test from the Ohio Department of Education to identify glitches and questions that need to be reworked for next year's test on the Common Core Standards. Having trouble keeping it all straight?

A veteran English teacher of 35 years with a master's degree, the author of two books on the writing process, and leader of college workshops took the test himself to see what his students would encounter. He discovered lengthy reading passages and difficult critical thinking questions all to take online. It took him several hours of concentrated effort to complete the test. He was curious to learn what scores he would receive so he'd have some sort of benchmark to best prepare his students. No feedback was available. He thought if a man of his qualifications and passion for English had difficulty, how will disengaged teens, mostly poor students, do? He said he'd rather spend class time on lessons he knows they can relate to and can handle.

The state instructs students to take a three hour test online with a high degree of difficulty. They are to be told the tests don't count and they will receive no results. They are encouraged to do their best to help the state perfect the test for next year.

Yeah right. Sure the kids are going to want to help the state out. A few kids will do their best, and the rest will give up when they see the test's length and difficulty. They barely do their best on work they can handle for credits toward their high school diploma. Most will finish in under a half hour and click *submit*.

I don't know what the state expects to learn from this pilot exam but I suspect they will find very poor results. What the education department should find out is that it is out of touch with the majority of students in public schools.

DAY 157
Lesson Plan

"Today you're going to learn the difference between a democracy and a republic, but first we'll take a survey of your favorite drinks." I thought I had a great plan for senior government today and was pleased that the kids perked up when I mentioned the drink survey. I always count on refreshments for a hook into a new lesson.

"Okay, we have 6 Cokes, 4 waters, 2 Gatorades, and 10 Mountain Dews. The majority chose Mountain Dew, so everybody has to drink Mountain Dew." Half the class groaned and again I was pleased. "You see, in a democracy, the majority rules. But if everyone gets their drink of choice, that's a republic. Even though we tend to label our government a democracy, we're going to get into groups and find parts of our Constitution that actually make it a republic. In the Pledge of Allegiance we don't say 'and to the democracy for which it stands', we say 'and to the republic for which it stands.'"

The kids bought into my lesson until Tony sauntered in late. Immediately I tensed and prepared for the worst. "Tony, please remove your headphones and put your iPhone in your pocket." He ignored me and roamed about the class talking and giving high-fives to his buddies. Shaq, JaQuan, and Wanyé found Tony more enticing than my lesson and within seconds I lost the class. Damn it, my beverage analogy couldn't even hold their attention.

"Tony, sit down. Be quiet everyone and let's continue. We're looking for guarantees in our Constitution that allow for everyone to choose their own beverage. Tony, sit down or I'm writing you up."

"Why you being so mean?" challenged Shaq. "We just havin' fun."

"Well, I'm having class, and if you don't like it you're welcome to a referral too. Now get in your groups of four and brainstorm Constitutional guarantees. Wanyé, put your phone away and join your group."

"Why you always talkin' to me?" he growled.

I faced my usual crisis. It did no good to send the troublemakers to the office since there would be no consequences. I had to live with them until the bell rang. Walking from group to group giving hints and suggestions, I saw very little work getting done. Only two groups generated any ideas at all, and my plan fell far short of my intention.

In the teachers' lounge at lunch, I released my anger and frustration with my colleagues describing my fizzled lesson. "Why don't you write a letter to the editor about disruptive students and a weak do-nothing administration," suggested Mr. Williams.

"Good idea," I said, open to a new plan. "I'll make school a republic alright. I'll choose my drink too. I just told the kids that Thomas Jefferson loved the ancient saying, *'The pen is mightier than the sword.'"*

DAY 158
Be Real

I unlock my door every morning at 7:30 and Robby's the first one in. I have to think what I'm doing with my six upcoming classes. I have notes to write on the board, the projector to set up, papers to run off, and email to answer. But Robby wants me to talk.

"How was your weekend?" or "How was your evening?" he offers.

"Fine," I reply. He really wants me to ask him about his weekend or night.

"Did you do anything special?" he persists.

"Not really." I'm annoyed with him because he's keeping me from my work. I'm annoyed with myself because he needs someone to pay attention to him. I know it's more important that I just stop and talk to him.

Who cares if I'm prepared or in control? The kids want me to be real. They won't remember the Treaty of Versailles or how many articles are in the Constitution, but they'll remember I told them I wanted to be a pro golfer or that I asked how they did in the track meet. I know all this and feel guilty for being curt to Robby.

I stop to reflect on my former teachers and what I remember from their classes. Sister Amelia fell asleep behind her desk in American history class. Miss Dressman spent most of the English literature class talking about her wedding plans. Father Stricker burped while interpreting the New Testament. Dr. Ames, my college French professor, threw erasers across the room and told us red wine was good for our health.

One year on a Friday, at the end of the final bell of the day, the kids taught me this dance called the jerk. Then weeks later during an assembly they called me to the stage to jerk to the music, and I did. The auditorium roared with delight and the kids talked about it for years. To this day they still beg me to do the jerk.

I decided to get real with Robby. I stopped fussing about and looked at him. "Did you get your hair cut?"

"Yes," he smiled, "I got tired of the Mohawk."

"It was getting a bit shaggy," I joked.

Just then Shaq entered the room. "Hey, Robby, that's a fresh hair cut. That's live."

Robby was in heaven because a cool kid complimented him. They started talking and I resumed my work, never so happy to see Shaq in all my life.

DAY 159
Letter to Sharice

Girl, are you so desperate for a boy to look at you that you are willing to settle for him? I see you in the hallway hanging on him, looking at him with glazed over eyes. You are so happy that you can't see the misery he will bring. I know what a jerk he is. He litters the floor around his desk and walks away. Just as easily, he'll litter you with his semen and walk away. Don't you know you're so much more than the object of some loser guy? You deserve a world of possibilities: homecomings, proms, a goodnight kiss from a gentleman, college, research papers, diplomas, a career, a wedding ring. Any day now your belly will be swollen and instead of a prom dress, you'll be wearing maternity clothes. Your sixteen-year-old life will consist of morning sickness, diapers, bottles, and crying in the night. Tell him to get lost, and come do your homework in my room.

DAY 160
Valuable Feedback

It's too hot for April. The custodian has not yet turned on the air. The weather is tricking the kids into thinking school is out. I have to open the windows and door to keep everyone from suffocating. From the windows, Interstate 75 traffic mixes with shouts of elementary children on the playground. From the door, middle school kids are slamming their lockers and using their outdoor voices.

"You're going to have to speak up and focus if you want to keep a breeze in here," I told my 9th graders. The heat had set into the room for the final bell of the day. "We'll go over the homework then review for our test on WWII. Moctar, start us off, number 1."

"I ain't answerin'."

"Do you want me to email your mom again?" I had just emailed her yesterday about his noncompliance. She replied it wouldn't happen again. I started the class with high hopes for Moctar's behavior, but he sat there with his lips shut tight. "Let's go, Moctar, or I'm contacting your mom."

He sprang up and flung his notebook across the room and pushed his textbook off his desk. "I'm fucking tired of you, fucking lame ass whore."

He circled about like a rabid dog then stormed out of the room. I called the secretary. "Moctar is on his way." I wrote down his exact words and sent Terrace to the office with the referral.

The next twenty minutes went pretty well. The kids became sober realizing that the line had been crossed. We went over the homework and started the test review. A couple of kids must have gotten brave again, for

I saw something fly across the room. I braced myself for another outburst. Ja'Quantez picked up something white and held out his hand. "It's only a piece of deodorant stick, Ms. Ball. You know it sure is hot in here."

"I couldn't agree more," I said, grateful that that's all it was and grateful for the end of the day.

When the kids were gone Moctar's words hit me hard. Never had such a strong string of profanity been directed at me. I assumed his punishment would be at least a 5 day suspension. The next morning the office email read: *Moctar Ibra has 2 days In School Discipline. Please send work.* Outraged I started towards the office. Then I hesitated. *Why don't I practice the principles of all those inspirational books I read? Dr. Wayne Dyer said you have something to learn from everyone. An enemy can be the best teacher.*

I asked myself, *What could I have done differently?*

1. Not called on him first.
2. Let him warm up and volunteer an answer.
3. Not threaten to call his mom in front of his peers.
4. Not back him into a corner.
5. Talk to him after class.

Dyer said, *Allow your ego to take a well deserved break.* Collecting Moctar's work I felt free and considered the possibility that just maybe I was a fucking lame ass whore.

DAY 161
Mechanics Malfunction

If I could have a dime for each spelling error I've circled on kids' essays in 30 years, I'd be a millionaire. I'm not talking about big words such as *political* or *constitution*, I'm talking about simple words I've taught to classes from the 6th to the 12th grades. Over and over I've explained the difference between *there (place)*, *their (possession)*, and *they're (contraction for they are)*. *Your* is possession and *you're* is a contraction for *you are*. *Our* is possession and *are* is a verb. *To* is a preposition and *too* means *also*. Did I dare mention a prepositional phrase? Forget *its* and *it's*. That would be like explaining the theory of relativity. My third grade teacher explained it like this: *its* is possessive. For example, *The bird broke its wing*. You wouldn't say, *The bird broke it is wing*. And *it's* is a contraction for *it is*. And apostrophes to show possession? Kids put an apostrophe on anything with an *s* whether it's possessive or not. *I have four brother's*.

Grammar must not be emphasized in the elementary grades anymore. If it is, I'm not seeing its effects. Kids don't even capitalize their own names anymore. I demand they capitalize all proper nouns until they become as famous as ee cumings.

What is really annoying is the misuse of *myself*. *Myself* is a stress or reflexive pronoun to be used only when the subject is *I*. *I treated myself to a hot fudge sundae*. *Jim treated me* (not *myself*) *to a hot fudge sundae*. Adults misuse it all the time too. I guess they think *myself* sounds more sophisticated than *me*. And could people please reply *You're welcome* instead of *No problem*. I didn't say anything was a problem. I merely said *Thank you*.

I hear cursive is out the door too, along with manners and respect. Soon I'll be out the door. I won't be a millionaire for all my red circles, corrections and disciplinary referrals, but I will take a modest retirement and my diagramed sentences with me.

DAY 162
Wake Up Call

I came to school this morning with a chip on my shoulder. I was holding a grudge against Dustin for making a scene in my French class yesterday afternoon. He wouldn't sit in his assigned seat and I sent him to the office.

"I'm sorry for yesterday," he said.

"Dustin, why do you act like a second grader in French class all the time? You're a senior and you say you're going to college next year."

"I don't like being with all those sophomores. They always correct me when I make a mistake."

"They didn't say a word to you yesterday. Class was just starting."

"I know. That's what I'm apologizing for."

Even though it was Friday I was in a foul mood. I was tired, and I guess it was last night's salmon and glass of wine at dinner that upset me. Instead of accepting his apology and focusing on first bell government, I kept raving about his behavior in French class.

Luckily for Dustin, Marisa entered the room and I renewed a grudge I had against her too. "You are never leaving my room again during class," I scolded. "Yesterday when I let you go to the nurse, you must have texted Trey in Mrs. Keller's room because there he went following you down the hall."

"I did not," she scowled incredulously.

Trey was right beside her and jumped to her defense. "I seen her in the hall and knew her stomach was hurtin'. I have the right to check on my girl."

"You were supposed to be in English, and I'm sure Marisa can walk 50 yards down the hall without you," I retorted.

Shaq was sitting there listening and had to throw in his two cents. "Man, Ms. Ball always has to make such a big deal out of nothin'."

Shaq really pissed me off and it was none of his business, but I recognized a thread of truth in what he said. Before my head and stomach burst, I decided to stop raving at everyone and begin class.

DAY 163
Poison

I was having a good first bell. All the kids bought into the chapter introduction on the judicial system. We had a nice discussion, and for the last fifteen minutes they were working quietly answering questions in their notebooks. I felt calm and satisfied. Then Tony barged in late as usual. He pranced around the room singing, talking, and patting his buddies on the back.

"Tony, sit down and get your book out. We're answering the questions on the chart board." He ignored me as usual and continued to distract his buddies. Not able to think for themselves, they joined Tony and the class fell apart. "Be quiet everyone and finish up before the bell rings," I yelled. "Tony, have a seat." He proceeded to the outlet over by the computers and started to charge his phone, talking and singing the whole time. "Tony, unplug your phone and sit down. The outlets aren't for personal use." He ignored me. "Go to the office."

"How you gettin' me in trouble with only two minutes left of class?"

"I don't care if there's two seconds left. Go to the office." I started writing his referral.

"Man, I gotta charge my phone and class is over anyway."

"Leave or I'm calling Officer Raby."

He stood at the door still entertaining his friends. I looked him in the eyes and pressed the call button. The bell rang and he left my broken class to torture his next teacher. I stormed to the office and slapped the referral into Mrs. Stein's hands. I returned to face my French class, angry, distracted, and physically shaken.

In ten minutes, one student negatively impacted not only me but dozens of other students. Over and over I ask myself why students are allowed to spread their poison day after day and why adults are not able to set up a firm discipline system and take control of their school.

DAY 164
Creativity Throughout the Years

The first word I can think of to represent *good* is *neat*. In the 50s we said, "That's neat." *Groovy* replaced *neat* in the 60s. Then we said *smooth* and *cool* up to the 90s. When I started paying attention to the students, I heard them saying something was *hard*. One day I was wearing a navy Izod jacket and was told it looked *tight*. *Beasty* was popular for a while, then came *amazing, gangsta,* and *sweet*.

Today, April of 2014, a group of bitchy girls, freshmen in my French class, said I looked *steak*. I assumed I looked bad and looked down at my clothes trying to remember what I had on. "What are you complaining about today?" I asked.

"No, Ms. Ball, *steak* means good," they said. "You know, like a steak is good."

Friday is dress down day and I guess they were referring to my jeans, t-shirt, and new sneakers. "Thanks," I said. "I wasn't expecting a compliment." They smiled at me reassuringly.

I jotted *steak* on my desk calendar so I was sure to capture the most creative word to date that I've heard for *good*.

DAY 165
Military Material

Mark joined the military. He missed the first two weeks of school because he was still in boot camp. His absence was excused, and, upon his return, I anticipated a new Mark, all in shape, responsible, and disciplined from his training. Eight months into the year, I've seen more of the old Mark than the new. He sleeps in class, rarely brings his materials, and has grades no higher than Ds. I can't understand his numerous uniform violations and behavior referrals. The military is all about conformity. He works the night shift at McDonald's and comes straight to school with a Red Bull. He's usually buzzed for the first 20 minutes of class, and then he crashes.

On the rare occasions that Mark is awake, he does share some pertinent comments. Today in government class we were discussing the military's new policy of allowing women in combat. Some students disagreed, since women are not as physically capable as men to carry heavy ammunition and support their fellow men in battle.

Mark stirred. "Some of the women I've trained with can pass the fitness tests alongside of the men. If they can meet the same standards, they ought to be allowed in combat."

"Thanks, Mark. That's interesting. It's good to have information from someone with firsthand experience."

"See, Ms. Ball. I think you should give me an A in this course because I'm in the military."

"Mark, if you're an example of what's in the military, this country is in deep trouble."

DAY 166
The State of the State

It's 8 a.m. and I walk back to my computer to take attendance. Half of the class is missing. This is not unusual. A fourth of the students will straggle in late and the other fourth won't show at all. I recall yesterday's faculty meeting. Teachers were informed that next year their evaluations will be based 50% on test scores and 50% on principal observations. The state has mandated that salaries, promotions, bonuses, and dismissals will be tied to these evaluations.

The observations are fine. The principal comes into my room and sees I'm up on my feet teaching. The students are under control and fairly engaged. I won't get penalized for that.

What bothers me is the other 50%, the test scores. Our status is tied to test results of kids who don't come to class. They have to be absent over 45 days for their scores to be discounted. So a student can be out of a class for 45 days and his score will be counted against a teacher. That's not all. If a teacher has a kid for first or second bell, but he comes to school later in the day, he's considered present, and his scores will count for the early classes even though he wasn't there. Theoretically, a student could be absent from a class for 100 days and his scores will count against a teacher. That is a possibility since there are no consequences for tardies at Madison High School.

I wonder what the state is thinking. It seems it's trying to fire teachers and/or discourage young idealistic and enthusiastic teachers from entering and staying in the profession. Holding teachers accountable for students not in the classroom is negligence beyond any irresponsible student or teacher behavior the state is trying to monitor.

DAY 167
Passing the Buck

Today I made it through first bell, Adrian and all. He was late as usual and I only had to tolerate him for around 20 minutes. I even made it through second bell French class with my bitchy freshmen girls. I ignored their rolling eyes, snide remarks, and huffy breaths and ended class with an impromptu game eliciting rare smiles from them. Third bell's a breeze, so I thought, as my honors seniors entered the room and began working on their current events.

Ten minutes into class, Adrian barged in and headed for Ami to conduct his social life. I heard the office call him to the In School Discipline room during second bell and wondered why he was loose. "Adrian, leave," I said. "This is third bell. You're in my first bell." He ignored me and kept talking to Ami. I raised my voice. "Adrian, get out of here now."

"No, you ain't doin' nothin' in here. I'm not hurtin' you."

I went to the call button by the doorway and pressed it. "Adrian Smith is in my room without permission and won't leave. Please send someone to remove him."

As I let go of the button, Adrian bolted for the door. "Fuck you," he yelled, and swatted my head with a handful of papers as he passed me.

I pressed the call button again and cried, "Adrian has just cursed me and swatted at my head." I went to my desk and wrote it all down. The secretary came to my door, and as I handed her the referral she said, "If this doesn't finally get him expelled…"

I had to return to the kids in front of me and, shaken and distracted, I still had to teach. How much more could be expected of someone, I thought.

Later, the principal sent an email to the faculty. *Adrian S. has been suspended for 5 days. As a senior we would like him to graduate and move on. Please allow him to complete any major assignments necessary to this end.*

I realized there would be no expulsion for Adrian, just more of the same ineffective punishment he's received for the past 12 years. Passing him out of a class, out of a grade level, and out of a school has been the pattern. No one has ever told him "no" and followed through. Let him disrupt classes all year long, swat and curse a teacher, then hand him a diploma. School has not taught him that actions have consequences. The administration just wants him out, with no skin off its back, to become someone else's problem out there in society.

DAY 168
Faking It

Ten minutes can be a lifetime at the end of a bell. Today I was at a good stopping point in French class. We'd finished the book exercises and I didn't want to pass out the worksheets but save them for tomorrow. I had to think fast. Letting them speak their usual inane English wasn't an option. Making them speak French was. The lesson was on clothing vocabulary and I had an idea.

"I'll take a volunteer to stand in front of the room and describe what you're wearing, in French of course." Dead silence. I picked up the worksheets. "Well then, I have just enough time to pass these out and explain your homework."

Deajah jumped up. "Je porte un pantalon noir et un polo rose."

"Très bien." I gave her a Jolly Rancher and a bonus point on my clipboard. "Who's next?" No one moved. I started to pass out the packets.

Marie came forward. "Je porte un t-shirt violet et un short blanc."

"Très bien," I said giving her the same reward. "Encore." Dead silence. I counted out 5 packets and lay them on the first desk in the first row.

I started for the second row when Robert rescued the class. "Je porte un jean et un blouson."

"Merci, Robert."

The kids finally caught on and we laughed each time I faked the homework. But in ten minutes almost everyone had performed. We got in some good oral practice and my worksheets were intact for the next day.

DAY 169
Hands-On Activity

Rarely do I miss a day of work, but I took advantage of a personal day on Friday, May 14. On Saturday morning I opened the newspaper to discover that my Madison High School students had made the front page. I read the article in disbelief. *Thursday evening at 10 p.m. four police districts responded to a 911 call from a Madison resident who reported kids breaking into the school. Dressed in black and wearing masks, they were attempting to pull off their senior prank. They planned to hang posters in the halls, put paper cups filled with water on the steps, and remove all the books from the library. One girl hid in the locker room and let the others in when the custodians left for the evening. Twenty students were arrested and twelve of those over eighteen spent the night in jail.*

What? Reporters are talking about the kids I've known for years. I was sure the students meant no harm. They thought they were carrying out a tradition. Last year's seniors broke in and toilet papered the school and moved the desks from every classroom into the auditorium. The only difference was they didn't get caught. I read further. Kristen, Sarah, Patrick, and Aaron were locked up? They spent the night in the Hamilton County Justice Center, the same place they toured just a few weeks ago as elite students?

I recalled April 27th, the day I took the four of them downtown to the Hamilton County Administration Building. The Rotary Club sponsored a youth and government day and invited teachers to bring their best seniors to participate in the daylong activities. It was extra work for me to make sub plans for all my classes, but I didn't want to deprive my students of this opportunity. Kristen has a perfect homework and attendance record, Aaron plays in the band and wants to be a music teacher, Sarah is president of National Honor Society, and Patrick always adds a spark to our political discussions. They deserved to go.

We arrived at the Administration Building at 8 a.m. to the enthusiastic welcome of the Rotary volunteers and were treated to a continental breakfast in which the kids delighted. Guest speakers took up the first half of the morning including Greg Hartman, Judge Ruhleman, and Dr. Odell Owens, the Hamilton County coroner. Dr. Owens had the audience spellbound with his use of statistics. "If children cannot read by the 4th grade," he said, "the higher the chance they have of being involved in a crime." Cities can predict how much jail space will be needed in ten years based on the 4th grade reading scores in a school district. High school diplomas are a must, as dropouts are most involved in crimes. "You can choose between a cap and gown or a body bag," he said. The best community service a teen can do is to find a child and teach him to read. He urged students to continue their education beyond high school—the higher the degree, the longer the life. According to statistics, PhDs live the longest. Patrick was the most excited about his talk. "I've wanted to see Dr. Owens in person for years. My dream just came true."

Role play filled the rest of the morning. Students were assigned names of commissioners, the staff, and the press to decide on the issue: *Should a senior center in Mt. Airy continue to operate with public funding or be privatized?* The students acted like highly functioning adults and it was easy to predict who the future leaders would be. Aaron and Sarah spoke on behalf of their teams and I was proud as they held their own compared to students from other schools. After the simulation everyone received a box lunch and a little break.

In the afternoon the students were given a tour of the Hamilton County Justice Center. The Rotary called it a "reality check." We saw the stark jail cells with only cots and toilets, and some of the inmates. The guide even showed us the food they eat called DBUs, Disruptive Behavior Units. For the first ten days, three times a day, inmates are given two big brownish orange biscuits, and that's it. They are made of oatmeal and ground vegetables and include all the necessary daily nutrients. They send the message that jail is no fun, yet uphold the 8th Amendment against cruel and unusual punishment. At the invitation of the warden, a brave chaperone tasted a DBU. The kids studied her carefully while she chewed it. "Not that bad," she said, "but not good either." One gaunt scraggly man in prison stripes passed our tour and said, "Stay out of trouble, guys." Amidst the grim surroundings the students were positive they would.

After the jail we went back to the Administration Building for a debriefing, raffle, and evaluation forms. The Rotary volunteers could not have been more supportive of youth and their future success. Driving back to school I felt pleased with myself for giving my students that hands-on experience. The next day we shared what we learned with the rest of the class. Dr. Owens' talk and the jail tour were especially popular topics.

Drama pervaded Madison High when I returned on Monday, May 17th. The seniors faced a ten day suspension, felony charges, and the withholding of their diplomas. After a week, the punishment was reduced to a five day suspension plus community service. When the kids were allowed back into the school they came to me for their missing work. I couldn't control my sarcasm. "It's been great fun reading about all of you in the newspaper."

"Get serious, Mrs. Ball," said Kristen. "I spent the night in jail crying and throwing up. I wanted to take it all back. I never expected our prank to turn out like that."

"Yeah," said Patrick, "last year the seniors did worse and didn't get nothing."

"True," I said, "but they pulled it off and you got caught."

"Go ahead," said Sarah, "and tell us your traffic ticket story."

Whenever the kids say something's not fair, I preach about the time I got an $80 speeding ticket but wasn't the only one speeding.

I continued to give them a hard time. "Patrick, I'm so glad to see that your idol Dr. Owens made such a lasting impact on you. I never thought you'd all be so inspired by the Rotary Club workshop that you'd want to experience the jail from the other side of the bars. I guess you were hungry for the DBUs."

"Mrs. Ball, can you just give us our work," said Aaron.

Actually, the seniors wouldn't have been so brave this year if last year's seniors had been punished. The administration knew who broke in last year but dismissed the whole affair. Rarely do I stick up for kids who get in trouble, but this time the administration, not the students, should have been found guilty for the Madison prank.

DAY 170
Pushing Buttons

It's Friday and community service projects are due Monday. In my syllabus, sent home the first week of school, I detailed the community service requirement for seniors and stated the school board policy. Fifteen hours of volunteering are required in order to graduate, as well as a 4th quarter project.

Shaq interrupted me as I was starting class. "Can we work on our projects this bell?"

"No, Shaq, I have a lesson for today. We've been talking about community service all year, and I gave out the project directions and rubric six weeks ago."

"Well, I already have an A in here, and you can't fail me if I don't do my project, can you?"

"Community service is a graduation requirement, Shaq. It's board policy."

"Then can we work on our projects now?"

"No, I'm having class. You had six weeks to write your essay and create your power point."

"You just want us to fail. You won't help us. You can't fail me if I don't do the project, can you?"

"I have been available to you all year in study session after lunch. You choose to talk and look at your phone every day instead of beginning your project."

My blood was starting to boil. I was getting trapped in a senseless exchange and I needed to stop. I turned my attention to the rest of the students, whom I'm sure didn't mind the delay. "Open to chapter 16, 'Power, Politics, and You.' We're going to read about retributive versus restorative justice."

"You won't answer my question," Shaq persisted. "You can't fail me if I don't do my project."

It was only 8:10 and I was hyperventilating. The air was foul in the room. Sean hadn't had a good hot soapy shower or clean clothes for days now. Angela brought in her rabbit to go with her project on animal rights, and the cage stunk. But the foulest thing in the air was Shaq's voice. "You won't answer my question," I heard him say, as I stared down at the filthy blanket covering Angela's cage.

"Shaq, I've already answered your question. What else is there to know?" My own voice, cracked and raised, betrayed any attempt at calm professionalism. *You are the adult here,* I told myself. *You come from opportunity. Stop arguing with a teen with little resource, save his own aggression.* "Our article begins on page 283. Ryan, read the first paragraph."

"I'm going to report you," Shaq interjected.

I opened my mouth to lash out at him, then realized I was letting him push my buttons. I needed to be pushing the buttons, inspiring and educating these kids in front of me.

"Did you hear me? I'm going to report you," he repeated.

I looked at him with my best innocuous expression. "Go ahead, Shaq. You have my permission to leave class right now and go down to the board office and report me. Meanwhile, we're reading 'Power, Politics, and You.'" Shaq sulked through the remaining forty minutes, and I completed the lesson I'd planned.

DAY 171
Off Course

I found out why Becky hasn't been doing well in government. She used to be one of my best students. Lately she's had her head on the desk and has been skipping assignments. Since I take everything personally, I thought she no longer liked me or my class.

This morning I saw her standing at her locker, t-shirt untucked and belly popping out. She was talking to a friend about "expecting" and a due date.

There went all my hopes for this cute-as-a-button blonde. I mentioned this to my coworker Emily who knows the scoop on all the kids. "Oh, yeah, she's pregnant."

"Who's the father?" I asked.

"Charles Lewis."

Emily could have named anyone but him. He was by far my all time most despicable student. Every day last year he would make his entrance to my class, walk about the desks, flirt with the girls, then sit down and call across the room to the guys about sports while I was trying to teach. If I kicked him out of class, the vice-principal would send him back within minutes. If I didn't call on Charles first every time, he would make a huge scene. I've never seen such disruptive and childish behavior from an 18-year-old. At field day last May, I threw a water balloon at him and said, "You were the biggest pain in the butt I ever taught." I got away with it since we were all out having fun.

"So that's who Becky is mixed up with. I had her future all planned out," I told Emily.

"What do you expect? Her mother is an alcoholic and doesn't give a damn about her. She has to find love somewhere."

"I love her. I had a scholarship, college, and a career waiting for her. And I envisioned a gentleman at the end of her hard work, someone who would value her as much as I did, not someone the likes of this kid."

Becky couldn't wait. She had to settle for Charles Lewis. She faces the beginning of her life as a single mother raising a child with no parents to support her. It's hard enough raising a child when two people are educated, well-off, and committed to their marriage. What chance does Becky have? She threw her looks, intelligence, and college away for a loser who considered her no more than another conquest. I was right there all the while and couldn't stop it.

DAY 172
All Is Forgiven

Shaq was in front of the class giving his community service presentation. I was in a pretty good mood because this was the culminating senior project and the last thing I had to grade. Moreover, I only had a few more days of him since he would soon be graduating. He was telling about all the snow he shoveled for free over the harsh winter. "One day I ended up shoveling the whole street," he said.

"Whoever heard of shoveling the street?" I asked.

"No," he corrected, "all the driveways on the street. I felt sorry for the old people who couldn't get out."

"That was a nice thing to do," I said. "I wish you would've been nice to me this year. I'm old too."

He laughed and went on to talk about volunteering at St. Rita's Haunted House and working at the concession stand for the wrestling tournament. He pointed to pictures on his 3-paneled poster then read his 400 word essay.

I noticed he didn't have his shoes on and was about to stop him and lecture about appropriate dress for a formal presentation. I restrained myself and let him finish.

"Community service benefitted me as well as others," he concluded. "I never thought I would do something for free and be okay with it. This requirement ended up giving me a feeling of satisfaction and accomplishment."

His classmates clapped but I frowned at him when he looked at me for approval. "Did I pass?"

"No Shaq, I'm afraid not." I pretended to write notes on his score sheet.

"You failed your project and won't be graduating." He looked at me panic stricken then with disdain, ready to accuse me of being the same bitch I'd been all year. I pointed to the floor. "You failed your project due to the holes in your socks."

He looked down at two big toes sticking out of bright green socks clearly in need of darning. We all had a good laugh before I called the next student to the front of the room. Oh, how fun and lighthearted I can be when I know it's ending soon.

DAY 173
Dirty D

The kids I teach have names such as Demetrius, Ja Keem, Tariq, Shanika, Tylea, Teesha, and Dirty D— not Brooke, Bradley, Courtney, and Blair. You can't assign a newspaper article for homework or a report. No newspapers are delivered to their doors and there is no bookcase of encyclopedias in their living rooms. They come to school wet when it rains, and they don't have braces on their teeth. They have tattoos, ankle bracelets, and grills.

Sixteen-year-old boys are fathers, and fifteen-year-old girls are mothers. They've lived with grandmas and aunts, they've been homeless, and they've slept in cars. They've witnessed murders, and they've been to juvenile jail called 20/20. Each Friday they bring me their court forms to sign verifying they've been in school all week. Their dinner may be sunflower seeds, potato chips, Mountain Dew, and Little Debbie Snack Cakes, while Brooke, Bradley, and Courtney are served grilled salmon, rice, and fresh asparagus.

They've been arrested, locked up, and even shot. They know the Miranda Rights and the meaning of big words such as *arraigned, incarcerated*, and *indicted*. So I don't need to teach them the chapter on the criminal justice system. Instead, they teach me rap songs and dances such as the Stinky Leg and the Jerk. They don't talk about college or who's going to be valedictorian. They care about relationships, entertainment, and survival.

One day Dirty D got on the Internet and showed me his incarcerated mother's mug shot and record of forgery, theft, and assault. Maybe that's why he holds the honor of being the only kid I've ever kicked out of class on his first day of school. Usually new kids are quiet and scope the place out for a few days. Not Dirty D, he started yelling across the room to someone the moment I assigned him a seat. "You will not control the atmosphere of my classroom," I said. "Go to the office."

I couldn't get rid of him though. The principal kept sending him back to me. I realized I had nothing to teach Dirty D, so I let him teach me. "What are the words to that rap song you sang when you jumped up on stage during our assembly last week?"

"You mean when I was freestylin? It go like this:

> *My name is Dirty D. I come from zone 15.*
> *I ain't pretty Ricky. I got on black Dickeys.*
> *Cause I'm tall, I play basketball.*
> *Can't call me wench. I don't ride the bench.*
> *Like D'Arius and JaQuan."*

I learned how to rap, and now I can do the Jerk. I promised the kids I'd let Dirty D teach it to me if they made it to school for an entire week. So on Friday I did it in front of the class while the music played and the kids filmed me on their cell phones.

"You're sick, Ms. Ball," said Dirty D.

"Sick? Is that what I get for being such a good sport?"

"No, sick means good," he said.

"Thanks, Dirty D. If you come to school Monday, you can teach me something else."

DAY 174
Off the Wall and Out of the Room

Randy has been one of my students on and off for five years. I taught him social studies in the 6th grade. He was friendly and loquacious then and I didn't think much more about him. When I was transferred to the high school I had him in my U.S. studies class as a 9th grader. He was still friendly and loquacious but frequently absent and turned in no work for four straight quarters to earn four straight Fs. This year I have him two times a day, study hall and integrated studies. Over the summer he turned into a monster. His friendliness turned into disrespect and defiance if I wouldn't let him out of the room to go to the nurse, the restroom, the water fountain, or just plain roam the halls. Randy was fine if I played best friend with him and talked about Led Zeppelin, AC/DC, Metallica, and System of a Down. But it was impossible to get him to do any work.

Truly, he is fun to listen to and joke around with as long as I'm not trying to get something done myself which is hardly ever. The other day I counted seven piercings on his face: two on his eyebrows, four on his ears, and one on his tongue. Trying to leave my work for a minute and give him some attention, I said, "I count seven piercings, Randy."

"No, no, Ms. Ball, I have eight, one on my nipple." He pulled up his shirt to show me.

I looked away. "I believe you, Randy."

The next day he came into my room. "I know, the number is eight," I said.

"Not no more, it's nine, one on my other nipple. And there's more other places but they're not school appropriate."

I pretended I didn't hear that and went back to work. A few minutes later Randy was at my desk. "Can I use the restroom? I have my planner. I signed it and he left the room. Fifteen minutes later he returned. "Sorry I took so long, I had to go do-do."

Randy is a sophomore in high school and has no credits to graduate so far. It is impossible to get serious with him, make him sit in his seat or do any work. All he wants to do is talk and goof off. Once he put his iPod at my ear and wanted me to listen to his friend's band. Then he asked me if I ever smoked marijuana. "Randy, I'm at work." If I were his neighbor, I could be so cool and fun standing in the yard and hanging out with him. But I'm his teacher.

"Where do you work?" I asked him.

"Gold Star Chili on Reading Road."

"I'm going to come there and bother you while you're trying to work and get you in trouble with your boss."

"My boss won't care, he's on crack."

There is no reasoning with him. He always gets the last word. "Randy, you are smart enough to be a prosecutor. You have a gift for talking and throwing people off guard so that they accidentally confess."

"My brain is too fried for that, Ms. Ball."

The next day he came to class with a tie-dye t-shirt wrapped around his head in a turban. He danced around the room and sang, "I'm a hippie Muslim."

"Sit down, Randy."

"My nipple hurts."

"Sit down," I said.

"I can't my butt's asleep." He went into the hall with Danny, an umbrella, and a wad of paper and started to play baseball. I wrote a referral and sent him to the office. I knew he'd be back in my room the next day. That referral was the eighth one I have written on him in a month. I wish I could just enjoy his goofiness but I don't have that luxury. I refuse to be one of those teachers you read about in the paper who is fired for having inappropriate communication with a student.

Today I kicked him out of study hall but I had to give him a fresh start in integrated studies. While we were reading *All Quiet on the Western Front* he made six different trips from his seat to the window sill to get Kleenex. I practiced my patience while he blew his nose dramatically each time. When it was his turn to read he read in a pronounced monotone to get a few more laughs.

"Out," I said. I wrote another referral. It read, *Please don't send Randy back to this room. I have no control over him. It is impossible to progress through a lesson with him in the room, and he ignores every direction I give him. This is my ninth referral just this month.*

DAY 175
Vietnam

When the Vietnam War was going on I was in my early twenties and too wrapped up in my golf career to pay too much attention to it. Besides, I had no brothers, and my boyfriend got a medical deferment. It was only through teaching about it in my U.S. history classes that I started to become interested in Vietnam. I learned that it was the longest war the U.S. ever fought and the only war the U.S. ever lost. 58,000 Americans and 4,000,000 Vietnamese died, and the U.S. spent $120 billion. Tens of thousands of veterans suffered from depression, drug addiction and post-traumatic stress. No matter how much money, how many bombs, and how many troops the U.S. poured into Vietnam, it couldn't break the determination of the Vietnamese to establish their own government. The 3.2 million tons of U.S. explosives actually lifted the spirits of the Viet Cong. They were willing to fight for 5, 10 or even 20 years. In 1973, U.S. troops pulled out and in 1975 Communist North Vietnam took over South Vietnam. Today it is one communistic country.

I give my students notes on all these types of facts, show slides, and assign a report. The kids have to interview either a veteran or a citizen from the Vietnam era. Since I didn't pay attention when I was young, I decided to interview a few veterans myself. Their information was first hand, unlike that in books from which I taught. It didn't contradict the text but made the war more real for both me and my students.

The year ends with Vietnam, the last topic on my American history syllabus. The following several days will tell the veterans' stories and how the kids and I connected with them.

I do not pretend that today's classroom is on the same grand scale as the Vietnam era, but I find it fitting that my endeavor ends here. For the Vietnam stories are a mixture of tragedy, defeat, senselessness, contradictions, courage, persistence, and finally, hope—not unlike these 185 days.

DAY 176
Primary Sources

To supplement my unit on Vietnam I had the kids interview a veteran or someone affected by the war. I told them that there are lots of people out there in their 50s and 60s, and to go find someone and talk to him or her. I gave them a checklist for their reports and twenty-five interview questions. Students brought in priceless reports containing the sadness of the loss of loved ones, disturbing descriptions of gory scenes, political information, and statements of courage, optimism, and faith. The following are excerpts from some of the reports.

"Dean Williams lost his leg as well as some good friends in an explosion near the Gulf of Siam."

"The worst experience for Jack Roberts was when people came back to the base with missing body parts."

"I interviewed James Martin, a bar owner with his liquor smell. Quick, quiet and ruthless, he was known as 'the snake' in Vietnam. 'People died directly in my face,' he said. 'When I got home I couldn't sleep. I had nightmares of being surrounded by those rice cake bastards. Hell, I couldn't even have sex with my own wife.'"

"John Hall started talking about a guy who stepped on a landmine and got his legs blown off and didn't die."

"We went through fields of human waste and I saw soldiers get shot and fall into the pile of crap and I would think, *why is this happening?*"

"I could hear the sounds of napalm dropping, the screams of children being burned alive, and bullets whizzing by my head."

"I was stationed at a secret base in Laos. I couldn't tell anyone where I really was. My family didn't find out until twenty years later. In Laos a woman and her child discovered us. To protect our base, I had to kill the mother and my partner had to kill the child. He never did get over that. My partner became a crack head and committed suicide five years ago."

"I saw the Viet Cong split a soldier's belly open and let the pigs eat it while he was still alive. 'Burnt in your brain' is how he described the memories of the war."

"But when you're looking through a scope, when you can see the color in their eyes, then they become a person and that makes it hard."

Mixed with the horrors was mention of good things that the veterans got from Vietnam.

"The best thing I got was that I was one of the lucky ones who got to come home alive instead of in a casket."

"It was by the grace of God that allowed me to come home safely."

"The best thing I got was the experience."

"People are just people throughout the world. We're all people no matter where we go in the world."

Vietnam was always depicted as such a hellhole that I was surprised by the descriptions of nature amidst the horror and destruction. Joe Sowder put it this way, "Just when I was in total despair and saw only evil in the world, I saw the most beautiful sunset one evening, absolutely beautiful."

"It was a beautiful country, the mountains, the swamps, and the jungles were all so pretty," another student's veteran reported.

The kids painted this extraordinary picture for each other and me. It was not a simple picture nor black or white. I was humbled by the wealth of historical experience held in this simple community. I was not the teacher with the knowledge. The students and veterans taught the Vietnam War.

DAY 177
Tammy

I was back at the computer entering the grades for the reports when Tammy came in my room. "Ms. Ball, I just wanted to thank you for assigning the Vietnam reports and my dad wants to thank you too." I just looked at her. I had written her off as yet another assignment not turned in. She usually had her head down during my class and all I ever saw was her long brown hair draped all over the desk. I didn't even know she was listening when I first assigned the reports or when the students were giving theirs. "Two weeks ago when I was working at Arby's my uncle came through the drive thru. I hadn't seen him in six years and I remembered that he was in Vietnam. I asked him if I could talk to him about Vietnam and he said, 'Vietnam, what's that?' He laughed and said sure. The next time he came through we set up a time when I could go to his place and talk."

"Where does he live?" I asked.

"Only four blocks from me."

"And you haven't seen him in six years?"

"My dad hasn't seen him in twenty-five years because of an old grudge they carried. I stopped going over there when my grandparents died. I was extremely nervous going to his house after so long so I asked my dad to go with me. We talked for three hours about Vietnam and other things. Because of you, my dad and uncle are reconciled and the whole family is going to start getting together."

"I'm glad, Tammy. If the assignment got your family together, that's good enough." I ventured, "Did you write anything down?"

"Yes, I took lots of notes."

"I will welcome a report from you anytime. Thanks for telling me your good news." I hugged her and went back to my computer work.

DAY 178
An Unlikely Reunion

Today was the last day of classes before final exams. I planned to do an intense review in my third bell U.S. studies class. Tammy came in my room before school started and set her report on my desk. I was annoyed. All my quarter grades were in and I didn't feel like reading any more reports or adjusting grades in the computer. Like a good teacher, I read it. It was eight pages long, well organized and written with correct grammar and punctuation. Not needing the corrections of my red pen, I found myself impressed with her writing ability and enjoying her long story, entitled *An Unlikely Reunion*. It contained priceless information about her uncle's experiences in Vietnam as well as her recent experiences with her family.

When she came to class I praised her work and asked if she would read it in front of the class. She agreed. Her speaking ability was as good as her writing. She rarely looked at her paper and uttered not one *um* or *a...* Here is how it ended: "As my father and I walked out of the room, I looked up and saw the family photo with my dad, my uncle, my grandma, and my grandpa. I was overcome with emotion, and, as the tears began to fall, my dad looked at me and smiled as he put his arm around my shoulder. Tuesday, May 19 will always stand out to me—the interview, the family reunion, the three hours of fighting back tears while my uncle shared details from the most important days of his life, and the one brotherly hug between my dad and uncle that marked the end of a twenty-five-year-old grudge. If it weren't for this assignment I would never have seized the opportunity to reunite my dad and his brother. Of all the assignments I've had this past twelve years, I believe this is the one I would not soon forget because of the circumstances. Once again, thank you Mrs. Ball."

I gave Tammy a 145% on her report and force passed her for the year in the computer. Before this I was discouraged and stale. I felt I was doing a terrible job with the kids and just going through the motions. I was even thinking about an early retirement. Then Tammy came in with her work (masterpiece) when I wasn't expecting anything from anyone. I decided I'd teach another year. The whole Tammy thing brought to mind my favorite golf quote, "Golf comes to you, you don't come to golf."

It disturbed me that Tammy was so bright but failing her courses. She was frequently absent and when she was in class I suspected she had her head on the desk because of her job at Arby's. "How late do you work after school?" I asked her.

"Until 11 p.m."

"I realize it's hard to do your assignments and stay alert in class, but you can't afford to blow off your credits with the excuse that you work. Tammy, if you don't get your high school diploma you'll be doing the same thing at Arby's when you're forty. You are one of the most talented students I've ever taught, and you should not accept an ordinary life and a minimum wage job."

She agreed and smiled, but I'm not sure I got through to her. She showed me a picture of her dad and uncle taken since their reunion. They both looked scraggly and the room they were in looked drab. The full reality of her circumstances hit me hard. I realized why her beautifully written report smelled of dog and cigarettes.

DAY 179
Parakeets and Rotten Teeth

War veterans are all around us though we may not realize it, men and women who served in WWII, Korea, Vietnam and Iraq. I had been teaching alongside a Vietnam veteran for seventeen years and it wasn't until recently that I discovered that he served in Vietnam. How could I not have known that? We were very good friends, ate lunch together, took the students on overnight camping trips every year, and gossiped practically every day at school. One day I mentioned that I was having my U.S. studies students interview a Vietnam vet, write a report, and give it to the class. The kids complained that they didn't know any veterans and were using that as an excuse to get out of the assignment. My colleague told me that he was a veteran and would be happy to let someone interview him. No one ended up using him for his or her report so I interviewed him myself. It was late May and he was retiring at the end of the year. I didn't want the wealth of information I knew he had to slip away.

John Gibson is 59 years old and retired from Madison School District after 30 years as a math teacher and guidance counselor. He lives in Cincinnati and was living in San Francisco, California in 1964 when the U.S. began sending troops to Vietnam. He enlisted in the Marine Corps. "I was in trouble and needed to straighten up," he said. "I was sent to Hawaii and Okinawa. It was in Okinawa that I found out we were going to Vietnam. We were the first ones there in 1964. I had no preconceived idea about Vietnam. We landed in boats because there wasn't even a landing field. We were going to build an airport."

Vietnam was worse than Mr. Gibson expected. The first thing he remembers upon his arrival is a captain who came out of the bushes with his head all bloody. "I have to be here a year," he thought. "If I have 364 more days of this, I'm not going home." He ended up in Vietnam for sixteen straight months. The first set of troops got extended because someone had to stay for the first rotation. "I was in Vietnam for two Christmases," he recalled.

Mr. Gibson's job was in communications. He was called a forward observer. His company explored the ground and told phantom jets where to observe VC activities. They would figure out the latitude and longitude coordinates so the jets could bomb the VC sites. They also searched for underground caves and destroyed them.

The war affected him in several ways. "Most of the servicemen were poor," he said. "I was going to get an education. I was the only one in my family who went to college. In the service there is a lot of downtime. All that time gets you thinking and stewing. I remember surfing the beach. You would do nothing for a month and then have three days of chaos, then go back to doing nothing. The downtime made me realize how lucky we are in America. It was so long ago, but I don't mind talking about it."

When Mr. Gibson returned home he thought he really lucked out by surviving Vietnam. Fifteen years later he was diagnosed with non-Hodgkin's lymphoma and discovered there was a strong correlation between Americans in Vietnam and this disease. U. S. planes sprayed Agent Orange over the countryside to kill the foliage so that the enemy could be detected. Dioxin was the deadly chemical in Agent Orange. "It was all around," said Mr. Gibson. He underwent cancer treatments and lost his hair and fingernails. "I got a little compensation from the government, but it was hard to prove that Agent Orange in Vietnam caused my cancer."

An injury he could prove was having a few teeth knocked out by getting hit in the mouth with shrapnel. For overall physical discomforts he recalls the heat and humidity, being dirty for weeks at a time, and drinking warm water. He will never forget the infamous sea rations. This was a packet containing six meals. A meal would include cigarettes, a can opener, chocolate, crackers, salt and pepper, and a can of dog food type meat. Parents sent cookies, and after a while we got hot meals that were better than sea rations. "We got mail from home. Some of the soldiers welcomed news and some soldiers didn't want to know, for example if their girlfriends were going to dump them."

The worst things he saw in Vietnam were farmers working in their fields then getting blown up in the middle of a war, and kids with no arms or legs. He also saw his pal's radio with a big hole in it. "It's hard when someone you know doesn't make it." He saw a lot of booby traps but didn't fall in any.

Mr. Gibson carried an M-14 rifle, a bayonet, a .45 caliber automatic pistol and an assortment of hand grenades. He didn't carry them all at the same time. It depended upon the assignment. It was like assessing what the weather will be like before a hiking trip and asking yourself, "What am I going to bring with me today?"

He described the enemy as weird. "You hardly ever saw them. They were nebulous. We called them 'Gook' or 'VC.' I didn't have any particular feelings about them. I just wanted to stay alive and go home. The Viet Cong didn't care about the Geneva Convention. Following the rules was a joke. If you're going to have a war, leave politics out, do what you have to do and get out."

John Gibson had no idea why the U.S. fought in Vietnam. "I don't remember knowing a thing." In 1964 the U.S. hadn't lost the war and he had no feel for where we were going with it. "I didn't feel good about it. I wasn't a hero when I came home." There was no party or parade for people coming back from war. Mr. Gibson lived in San Francisco in the midst of hippie land. "I didn't want anyone to know I was in Vietnam. I was in the closet. The war protesters were at the airport. I didn't worry about them; I just wanted to go home."

"People in the world don't think highly of the U.S. We're in everyone's business. The politicians try and sell the war to the public by saying we fight to protect our freedom. It's really about money and power. What makes it worse is that politicians try and be politically correct in running the war. You can't be politically correct in wartime. Politicians won't let the generals run the war. It's like the board members of a school running a football game and not letting the coaches call the plays. But if you join the army you have to fight. I feel like I got used. But what did I know at nineteen?"

Iraq is turning into another Vietnam according to Mr. Gibson. One difference is that during Vietnam people weren't as gung ho about supporting the troops. For Iraq there is a conflict between supporting our troops and supporting the war.

For Mr. Gibson, Vietnam is a study of opposites. The country was so pretty and green yet so devastated by Agent Orange. There were bright green, orange and yellow parakeets alongside of kids all wearing black with rotten teeth. Vietnam gave him his education and appreciation for the U.S.; yet it gave him cancer and made him skeptical about U.S. politics. His mom made him a scrapbook filled with pictures and articles about his sixteen months in Vietnam. It is the only artifact he has from the war and represents his life changing experience. "It made me who I am," he said.

DAY 180
History Alive

Gary Jones is a Vietnam veteran who belongs to my golf club. He is 59, has a wife and two daughters, and owns his own business. I caught him after his golf game on a Wednesday afternoon in the club tavern having a drink with his partners. Ambitious for one more interview to share with my students to wrap up our unit on Vietnam, I asked him if I could talk to him about his service. He took his beer and cigarettes to an empty table in the corner of the room and told me he's done this before for his nephews and to ask away. I told him I was interviewing him with utmost respect and humility since I was totally ignorant of real war. He rolled his eyes and shrugged off my disclaimer.

Did you enlist or were you drafted into the military?

I enlisted to avoid the draft. I was eighteen and one of 11 children and didn't have a dime to go to college. If you enlist you can control your assignment. I chose military intelligence and went to training camp in Ft. Jackson, SC. I took a twelve-week crash course to learn the Vietnamese language and went on a one-year tour of Tokyo, Philippines, Okinawa, Thailand, and Saigon.

How did you feel about going to Vietnam?

In 1965 Vietnam wasn't a big thing. I was a naïve kid who listened to the Beach Boys and liked to work on my car. I had no idea what was going on in Vietnam. When I got there I thought I was going to do basic field interrogation and I felt deceived by the reality of the whole thing. On the field in Vietnam we captured prisoners and held them for one day. The assignment was called basic intelligence and initial interrogation. That's where my language training came in. We asked them, "Who is your commanding officer? Where is the rest of your company?" We beat the shit out of the enemy to get them to talk.

What did beating the shit out of them consist of?

We gave them flying lessons. We put two in a helicopter and took them up. If one didn't talk, we'd throw him out. The other sang like a bird... (Gary looked at me almost as if to apologize.) *It was a different time.*

In what ways were you affected by the war?

I lost my naivety and I lost my humanity. We treated those people like dogs. We learned to hate them. It was the culture... I also learned to drink in Vietnam. I didn't drink a drop before then. There were the "drinkers" and the "heads." The drinkers drank and the heads smoked marijuana.

I read many accounts of Vietnamese atrocities towards Americans. Why are you only telling of American atrocities towards the Vietnamese?

I'm sure there were. But personally, I didn't see atrocities towards Americans.

Do you mind talking about Vietnam or would you rather keep it in the past?

Keep it in the past. You put your time in and got the hell out. Anyone who reenlisted was suspect. We had nothing to do with the lifers. They sold out to the establishment.

What was the worst thing you saw in Vietnam?

My good friend got killed. We were in the same company. We were in our tin roofed huts when there was a rocket attack. There was no warning, for rockets are on you right now. His name was Tom Carter from South Dakota.

Were you ever wounded?

Yes, I got shot in the back. I thought I was dead. I lay there screaming like a girl. When soldiers get hurt, they scream. It's not like on TV or in the movies. Real screams in real war have a different sound. The only movie that comes close is Full Metal Jacket.

What about *Saving Private Ryan* **or** *Born on the Fourth of July*?
He gave those movies the finger.

What was the best thing you got from Vietnam?
I got four years of college from it. The GI Bill is the greatest thing ever. I went to UC and majored in business.

What daily physical discomforts stand out in your mind from Vietnam?
The crushing humidity. Your clothes rotted in your duffel bag. The latrines were terrible, the showers were terrible, and the food was terrible. There was no refrigeration. We got drunk on warm cheap beer like Iron City.

What weapons did you carry?
I carried a .45 caliber pistol which wasn't much, and a M79 grenade launcher which could do some damage.

Did you kill people?
Yes. His eyes told me he was finished with that question.

How did you feel towards the North Vietnamese?
We hated them all. We called them "Gooks, Mother Fucking Gooks."

Did you call the enemy "Charlie?" I read that in my History Alive program that I teach from.
"Charlie" were the Viet Cong in the South. I was stationed in the North. We fought conventional warfare v. the guerilla warfare of the South. So I had no experience with the booby traps and punji stakes that Charlie devised. They dug holes and hammered in pointed stakes. Then they shit on them and covered them with brush. American soldiers would fall into the traps and land on the stakes and die a slow painful death.

Do you communicate with any of your Vietnam buddies today?
Just letters and Christmas cards.

Why did the U.S. fight in Vietnam?

At 18 years old I didn't know. I had a vague idealistic idea about stopping the spread of Communism, but I didn't think beyond that. Now at 59 years old, I think it was about money, power and control.

How do you feel about fighting in the only war the U.S. ever lost?

Vaguely betrayed. It was so unnecessary. Whenever I'm in a stadium that holds 57,000 people, I look around and say to myself, "This is how many people died for some fat ass politicians?"

Do you think the U.S. efforts were in vain?

Absolutely.

Should the U.S. be praised or condemned for its actions in Vietnam?

Condemned.

How did Vietnam affect the U.S.?

It opened the floodgates to question authority.

How did Vietnam affect the world?

It showed that the U.S. wasn't the all-powerful entity it thought it was.

How did you feel about the war protesters?

I hated them, all the privileged bastards at home. I'll never watch a Jane Fonda movie. That was totally disrespectful when she posed on the seat of an anti-aircraft gun in Hanoi. Then I got spit on in Seattle coming from my first hitch in '68. Some long-haired little bastard said, "Hey soldier boy, what's all that shit on your chest?" I just said 'fuck you.'

Do you have any artifacts from Vietnam?

I gave all my medals to my nephew. I got the Purple Heart, the Good Conduct Medal, the Combat Infantry Badge, and the Vietnamese Service Medal. The only thing I have is a dummy hand grenade that I use as a paperweight.

Have you visited the Vietnam Memorial in Washington?

Yes. Ten years ago. I took my nephew. I saw my friend's name, Thomas Carter.

How did it feel to look at the memorial?

Sad. I look at all that black marble, all that waste of humanity.

What stands out most in your mind about Vietnam?

Dirt.

In light of Vietnam, how do you feel about U.S. involvement in Iraq?

I'm a republican, and I initially supported Iraq. Now I think it's another Vietnam.

Gary looked at his watch and asked if I was done. He had to get back to his business. I thanked him for talking to me. *"It was no big deal,"* he said. *"My experience was no different from anyone else's who served in Vietnam."*

DAY 181
Senior Letters

Each year at the end of the last quarter Mrs. Keller, the English teacher, requires her seniors to write letters to each other and to teachers of their choice. Sometimes, if I'm lucky, kids will think enough of me, and letters will appear in my mail box. I'm including two of my favorites to brag how I'm viewed by the good kids.

Mrs. Ball,

I remember the first time I met you. It wasn't in 9ᵗʰ grade U.S. history. It was in 7ᵗʰ grade. Me, Hawa, Sanoma, and Julia were in the middle school bathroom being loud, and you were teaching class across the hall. You came into the bathroom and told us to be quiet because you were trying to teach. I was really embarrassed because I wasn't playing. I really went to the bathroom. Then when 9ᵗʰ grade came along I had your class. I thought you were going to be a mean teacher. But I found out you weren't.

I loved being in class with you. You made it such a wonderful place to be. Real relaxed, and you could be at ease and not feel stupid if you got an answer wrong.

I like how you always have the day planned out. You just know how you're going to do it. Step by step. Each chapter and article and the timing is always right. I like that kind of structure. I always look forward to doing your work. It's wonderful. I can always look forward to coming to your class for government. It's so peaceful. I know what I'm doing and I feel good enough to give up my answer. I'm really going to miss you and government.

I remember having government in 3rd grade with Mrs. Adams. I knew I liked it then but you just made me love it more. If I had to take a course over again, it'd be government. It's a class you can relax in and do your work. I can't really describe it.

(What I secretly appreciate is that you don't let anything slip past you.)

Sincerely,
Angela M. Ellis

DAY 182
Why I Teach

Senior Letter #2

Dear Mrs. Ball,

I want to thank you for being my social studies teacher for three years. You had my sister when she was in the sixth grade. Then you had me freshmen, sophomore, and senior year. I know that I was a goof-ball in ninth grade. Brittany and I would always fool around. I know we gave you a hard time and I want to apologize for it. To this day I don't know why I acted like that and when I think of it, I feel ashamed of myself. I have also heard that your freshmen classes this year are getting to you. The group of freshmen this year is pretty annoying. I feel bad for you really, but we only have a few more days left of school. So hang in there.

In ninth grade I remember getting kicked out into the hallway a lot and just getting on your nerves. I was a horrible student and I suddenly realized that I needed to grow up. Again I would like to say sorry for all the troubles I have put you through. You are a great teacher and I will always respect you for that. I appreciate all the hard work that you have put into teaching our class.

My sophomore year was a way better year. I had the perfect notebook and would always have my homework with me. That year was probably our best year together.

I wish I could have had you for a junior teacher too. I missed you so much last year. Now, my senior year, I know I haven't been as focused on school work as much as I need to be. I know that I still try as hard as I used to. I just don't have any time after school to do homework. I have held a job all year and that is the reason I have fallen asleep in your class a few times. I know all of my problems in your class are due to *having too many after school activities. I just wanted you to know the reason why my behavior changed and I'm sincerely sorry for not giving my all to your class this year.*

You are the most fun and up-lifted person I know. You get so into the topics that we talk about in class. I love your teaching style. It's so fun. I think it's so funny how our class will fight over trying to get stamps. No other teacher does the stamps so that makes you unique. You are also the only teacher who has us write on the board to go over our homework. I love this technique because it helps my brain get engaged in the work and I actually like learning in your class. You have given a whole new meaning to teaching in school. You know how to be fun.

I want to let you know that you will be in my thoughts well after high school. Even though we've had some disagreements this year, I will miss you and always love you, Ms. Ball. I'll never forget when you got on stage and started dancing. Watching you do the Jerk was awesome. You are a very brave woman for getting up on that stage and showing your moves to the entire school. You made everyone's day and that was great.

I know you love golfing so I hope everything goes well with the tournament, and make sure you don't get hit in the eye with a golf club again. I remember when you came to school with a black eye. You must be a tuff woman because that looked like it hurt.

You have taught me so much including how to grow up. I will always remember and love you. You are a very special person and have impacted my life in a positive way. When I'm gone next year and going to nursing college, I'll be thinking about you.

Love you,
Jamie

DAY 183
Cotton Candy

Many school districts are emphasizing better nutrition in their cafeterias while feeding students a diet of cotton candy in the classrooms. Of the 185 school days each year, at least 20 are lost to non-academic activities scheduled during valuable class time. The pastel puffy treat presented to kids at the beginning of the year leaves only a mouthful of sugary grains at the end.

Student Council meetings, Spirit Week, homecoming and prom activities, Awards Day, pep rallies, and Field Day are a few of the ingredients that shorten bells or cancel classes altogether. Fire and tornado drills, lockdowns and pranks interrupt class just when teachers and students are engaged in their work. Three whole days are wasted before Thanksgiving, Christmas, and Spring breaks due to the nonsense festivities of Turkey Bowl, Midday Madness and Spring Fling. It seems January and February would be a good time to get down to business, but the vacation attitude prevails with snow days and two three-day weekends for Martin Luther King and Presidents Day.

If schools want to improve test scores they can do it without spending a cent. Eliminate the fluff. If teachers are responsible for covering a certain amount of material and for student achievement, give them at least a chance with their students—more time and less distractions. If U.S. schools want to be the best in the world, the party atmosphere must change to a learning environment. Students need good nutrition. It's called "academic learning time" in educators' jargon. Cotton candy can be served one day at the end of the year as a reward for everyone's accomplishments.

DAY 184
There's Always Hope

My niece, Kimberly, just graduated from Boston College summa cum laude. To earn that honor a student must rank in the top 4.5% of the class. At her graduation party she told me about her friend, also a summa cum laude, who is going to Harvard graduate school for a one year program in elementary education, administration, and research. Although Kimberly's friend is a brain and could make a lot more money in the fields of business or technology, her passion is children and to influence the course of their education.

This story gave me two simultaneous reactions. Oh, why is this girl wasting her intelligence on such a futile endeavor? And, yeah, that's exactly what education needs—bright, young, and idealistic professionals, so perhaps in the future, some of my most negative days of reporting will never again be necessary.

DAY 185
Empty Nest

The kids are gone for the year. Today is a teacher work day, my last day. I enter my classroom to finish what I couldn't get done with them in the room. I still have grades to finalize, curriculum maps to write, and ordering to do.

I look around. The desks are wiped clean of pen and pencil smudges, eraser bits, and obscene graffiti. Nick's desktop, front seat middle row, shows no signs of his obsession with fancy cars, Maserati, Lamborghini, Ferrari. The custodians have vacuumed the broken crayons, sunflower seeds, gum wrappers, and fingernails from under the computer tables. Every day I saw the debris and meant to remove it myself but couldn't get to it.

How innocuous and promising everything looks. The learning objectives I carefully printed with markers on sentence strips speak purposefully from the bulletin board. The three big mouths, Will, James, and Eric, aren't here to mess up my otherwise bright and well-behaved world studies class. I set to work in my quiet, clean, empty room and think, *I could actually teach if it weren't for the kids.*

People keep asking me when I'm going to retire. I say I'm not sure. What I'm sure of is that I'll go inconspicuously. I hate parties and all those emotional goodbyes. I'm 66 and can go whenever I want, but now my golf game is so lousy, I'm not even local tournament material. I may as well hang around. Teaching is all I know.

I can't part with the Iwo Jima poster I created, the Gandhi movie, or the CD of Kennedy's speech at the Berlin Wall. These represent my finest teaching moments—the day I held the whole class spellbound as I recounted the Cuban Missile Crisis.

But should I step aside for the young and idealistic teachers, more in touch with today's culture? Maybe I'll delight in a new and free lifestyle. Or maybe I'll be lost and bored and regretful of my decision, facing long days with no kids, administrators, or politicians to complain about. I don't have an answer today. Whenever I can't make a decision, my daughter says, "Mom, you'll know it, it'll be obvious."

It's not obvious yet. So after I close down my room and leave here, I'll carry out my year-end tradition. That is, I buy myself a gift, a significant one. Teaching is so damn hard I reward myself for surviving yet another school year. Two years ago I splurged on diamond earrings. Last year I went straight to the pro shop for new golf clubs. Later today I'm taking this assignment to a publishing company and making a deposit on *185 Days: School Stories.*

About the Author

Linda Ball is a teacher with 30 years experience at the elementary, middle, and high school levels. She holds two master's degrees from the

University of Cincinnati, one in education and one in French literature. She lives in Cincinnati, Ohio, with her husband Jim. They have one daughter PJ, also a teacher. Linda confesses her passion is not teaching and writing, but golf. She aspired to play the LPGA Tour in the early 70s, but failed to qualify. As an amateur she has won a City Championship and 18 Club Championships. She is currently teaching high school French in Cincinnati. With this, her first book, she hopes in some small way to influence the direction of public school education.